Winning Recipes!

by

Bruce & Lee Fischer

GOLDEN WEST ☼ PUBLISHERS

Note: Betting terms, payoffs and rules, etc. vary from casino to casino. Ask your dealer or casino representative for clarification of any specific questions you may have.

Printed in the United States of America

ISBN #1-885590-02-4

Golden West Publishers, Inc.
4113 N. Longview Ave.
Phoenix, AZ 85014, USA

(602) 265-4392

A
♦

Table of Contents

Breakfasts

Appetizers

Salads & Soups

Breads

Main Dishes

Side Dishes

J ♣

Desserts & Drinks

🎲🎲 Gambling Information 🎲🎲

J ♣

Breakfasts

Huevos Rancheros
Breakfast Eggs—Mexican style

4 CORN TORTILLAS
REFRIED BEANS, heated
4 EGGS
1 cup GREEN CHILE SALSA, heated
4 oz. LONGHORN CHEESE

Heat tortillas very briefly in oil. Drain and keep warm. Place tortillas on a baking pan and layer with refried beans. Fry eggs in butter until whites are set but yolks are still soft. Place one egg on each tortilla. Spoon salsa on top and sprinkle with cheese. Place under broiler until cheese melts and yolks are cooked to taste. Serves 4.

Blackjack's origins are European, though it's uncertain just what game is the direct ancestor. Blackjack is a nickname for the game of twenty-one. The nickname arose because early casinos paid a bonus on a hand consisting of the ace and jack of spades. The combination was dubbed a blackjack.

Lucky Eggs Chorizo

1/2 lb. CHORIZO
1/4 cup diced ONION
2 med. RED POTATOES, diced
4 lg. EGGS

1/4 cup MILK
4 (10-12 inch) FLOUR
TORTILLAS

Crumble chorizo and fry in skillet until done. Drain well and set aside. Put onions and potatoes in skillet, cover and cook over medium heat until potatoes are tender and onions limp and slightly browned. In a small bowl, beat eggs with milk. Add to skillet and scramble until eggs are cooked. Add sausage and stir well. Place equal amounts of mixture on each tortilla, roll up and serve. Serves 4.

Jack Cheese Omelet

1 cup diced MONTEREY JACK CHEESE
4 slices BACON, cooked and crumbled
4 EGGS
1/2 tsp. SALT
1/4 tsp. PEPPER
pinch BASIL
pinch OREGANO
2 Tbsp. MILK
2 tsp. BUTTER

Combine cheese and bacon in a small bowl. In another bowl, place the balance of the ingredients (except butter). Beat with fork to blend. Heat one teaspoon of butter in 6-inch skillet. Pour in half of egg mixture. Cook over medium heat, lifting edge of omelet to let uncooked egg run down into pan. When top is softly set, sprinkle with 1/4 of cheese mixture. Fold omelet over filling and slide carefully out of pan onto ovenproof plate. Sprinkle with 1/4 of cheese mixture. Make second omelet the same way. Place both omelets in 400° oven for 5 minutes (or until cheese melts). Serves 2.

Daily Double Shirred Eggs

4 CUSTARD CUPS
softened BUTTER
4 EGGS
4 Tbsp. MILK or CREAM
SALT and PEPPER to taste
PAPRIKA for garnish

Butter insides of custard cups. Put one tablespoon milk (or cream) into each cup and add one egg. Season with salt and pepper. Set cups in a shallow pan and pour hot water (about 1-inch deep) around cups. Bake at 325° for 15 minutes. Top with dash of paprika and serve. Serves 2.

Orange on Orange Pancakes

2 cups BISCUIT MIX
2 Tbsp. grated ORANGE RIND
1 cup ORANGE JUICE
1/3 cup MILK
1 EGG

Combine ingredients in bowl. Mix until moistened but still lumpy. Heat and lightly grease griddle. Pour 1/4 cup batter for each pancake and turn once. Serve with *Orange Syrup.* Makes 8 pancakes.

Orange Syrup

1 1/2 cups LIGHT CORN SYRUP
1 can (6 oz.) FROZEN ORANGE JUICE CONCENTRATE

Thaw orange juice (do not dilute). Mix corn syrup with concentrate until well blended and warm. Serve with pancakes.

Silver Dollar Pumpkin Pancakes

1 cup SELF-RISING FLOUR
1 Tbsp. SUGAR
1/2 tsp. CINNAMON
1/4 tsp. NUTMEG

3/4 cup MILK
3/4 cup PUMPKIN
2 EGGS

Mix first four ingredients together. Whisk balance of ingredients together and add to flour mixture. Pour silver dollar size pancakes on hot, greased griddle. Makes 36 pancakes.

Gamblers Waffles

3 cups FLOUR, unsifted
6 tsp. BAKING POWDER
1 tsp. SALT
2 tsp. SUGAR

6 EGGS
2 1/2 cups LIGHT CREAM
1/2 cup BUTTER, melted

Mix flour, baking powder, salt and sugar in a large bowl. In a small bowl, beat egg yolks until light in color and add cream and butter. Add mixture to dry ingredients and stir to mix well. Beat egg whites until stiff peaks form and fold into mixture. Bake in waffle iron. Serve hot with fruit sauces or syrups. Makes 6 waffles.

Raisin-Cinnamon Pancakes

1 cup MILK
1 EGG
1 Tbsp. VEGETABLE OIL
1 cup packaged PANCAKE MIX
1/2 cup RAISINS
1 tsp. ground CINNAMON
BUTTER or MARGARINE

Preheat non-stick skillet over medium high heat. In medium bowl, mix milk, egg and vegetable oil until well blended. Stir in pancake mix, cinnamon and raisins. Pour 1/4 cup batter, into skillet and cook until each side is lightly browned. Makes 8 medium sized pancakes.

Chemin de Fer French Toast

12 slices CINNAMON BREAD
1/2 cup BUTTER or MARGARINE, melted
4 whole EGGS
2 EGG YOLKS
1/2 cup SUGAR
4 cups HALF-AND-HALF (or 3 cups MILK and 1 cup
    WHIPPING CREAM)
1 Tbsp. VANILLA

Brush both sides of bread with melted butter and place in buttered 9 x 13 pan. In large bowl, beat eggs and egg yolks together. Stir in sugar, milk, half-and-half and vanilla. Pour mixture evenly over the bread slices. Bake at 350° for 25 minutes (tops should be lightly browned). Cut into squares and top with syrup, fruit or, try one of the toppings below.

Aces High Cinnamon Topping

1 tsp. CINNAMON   6 Tbsp. BUTTER, melted
4 Tbsp. BROWN SUGAR   1/1/2 cup NUTS, chopped

Combine ingredients and serve.

Deuces Low Walnut Topping

1/3 cup BROWN SUGAR   1 tsp. CINNAMON
1/4 cup WHITE SUGAR   1 cup WALNUTS, chopped

Mix all ingredients together and serve.

High Roller Spanish Eggs

1/4 cup CORN OIL
1/2 cup diced GREEN BELL PEPPER
1/2 cup diced ONION
1 cup chopped TOMATO
1 tsp. BLACK PEPPER
1 can (4 oz.) diced GREEN CHILES
6 EGGS
1 cup grated MONTEREY JACK CHEESE
SALSA & CORN TORTILLAS

In a microwaveable dish, mix together the first six ingredients. Cover and microwave on High for 5 minutes. Stir mixture and then break eggs over top. Pierce each yolk and egg white at least once with a toothpick. Sprinkle cheese on top. Cover and microwave on High for 3 to 5 minutes or until eggs are done. Let stand for 3 minutes. Serve with warm corn tortillas and a side of salsa. Serves 4.

Quick Start Eggs

1/2 cup chopped ONION
1/4 cup chopped GREEN PEPPER
2 Tbsp. BUTTER
3/4 cup grated CHEDDAR CHEESE
4 HARD-BOILED EGGS, chopped
4 ENGLISH MUFFINS, split

Sauté onion and green pepper in butter. Add cheese and eggs to pan and stir. When cheese mixture is well heated, spoon over toasted muffins. Serves 4.

Blackjack Anyone?

A Glossary of Blackjack Terms

Ace—The ace may be counted as a one or as an eleven-value card. Two's through nines are counted at their face value.

Blackjack—**1.** The name of the card game, also called Twenty-one.

2. An instantly winning hand. The two first cards dealt consist of an ace and a 10, jack, queen or king.

Burning a card—The removal of the top card from a deck by the dealer and placing that card face up at the bottom of the deck.

Bust—To draw a card that puts the total of the hand over 21.

Double Down—The player chooses to turn both cards up, double the original bet and play both hands.

Hit—Drawing more cards to the original hand of two to bring the hand count as close as possible to 21.

Hole-Card—The dealer's card that is dealt face down.

Insurance—If the dealer's first upcard is an ace, the player may "buy insurance" (place an additional bet that the dealer **has** a blackjack).

Natural or Blackjack—First two cards dealt are an ace and a 10-value card, forming a blackjack.

Push—A tie between the dealer and player, in which both have identical totals or blackjacks, with neither side winning the bet.

Soft Hand—A hand counting the ace at its 11 value. For example, a hand consisting of an ace and a 7 is a soft 18.

Splitting Pairs—Separating two cards of equal rank, such as aces or 9s, turning them both face up, matching the original bet, and drawing to these cards as two individual hands. All 10-value cards are considered pairs for the purpose of splitting.

Stand pat—Player refuses a hit (does not want additional cards).

Ten-value card—10's, jacks, queens and kings are ten-value cards.

Appetizers

Ante up Mushroom Turnovers

1 pkg. (8 oz.) CREAM CHEESE
1 1/2 + cups all-purpose FLOUR
1/2 cup plus 3 Tbsp. BUTTER
1/2 lb. MUSHROOMS, chopped
1 lg. ONION, diced fine

1/4 cup SOUR CREAM
1 tsp. SALT
1/4 tsp THYME
1 EGG, beaten

Beat cream cheese, 1 1/2 cups of flour and 1/2 cup of butter until smooth. Shape into a ball, wrap with wax paper and refrigerate 1 hour.

In a skillet (medium heat), melt 3 tablespoons of butter, add minced mushrooms and onions and sauté until tender. Stir in sour cream, salt, thyme and 2 tablespoons of flour. Set aside.

On floured surface, roll half of the dough to 1/8-inch thickness. Cut into 1 3/4-inch circles with cutter. Place mushroom mixture on one half of the circle, brush edges with egg and fold in half. Press edges with fork to seal and prick tops. Place on ungreased cookie sheet and brush with remaining egg. Bake at 450° for 12 to 14 minutes.

Makes 3 1/2 dozen.

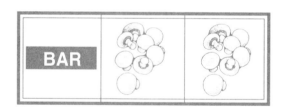

Quick Tortilla Delights

Place **FLOUR TORTILLAS** under broiler until warm. Spread with melted butter and sprinkle generously with grated **LONGHORN CHEESE**. Add **diced ONIONS AND CHILES**. Return to broiler and heat until cheese melts.

Shrimp Stuffed Artichokes

2 - 4 ARTICHOKES
1 pkg. (16 oz.) frozen BAY SHRIMP
1 cup sliced CELERY
2 Tbsp. LEMON JUICE
1/2 cup MAYONNAISE
SALT and PEPPER to taste

Boil artichokes, cool and chill. Defrost shrimp, mix with remaining ingredients and chill. At serving time, gently push artichoke leaves outward, fill with seafood mixture and serve with dressing of choice. Serves 2.

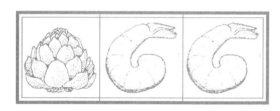

Go for the Green Guacamole

2 med. AVOCADOS
1 Tbsp. JALAPEÑO, fresh or canned, diced
2 Tbsp. fresh CILANTRO, diced
1 tsp. GARLIC SALT
1 med. TOMATO, chopped
1 tsp. LIME JUICE

Mash avocados in a medium sized bowl and add remaining ingredients. Blend well. Makes 1 1/2 cups.

Pizza Lovers Tortillas

2 lg. FLOUR TORTILLAS
1/2 cup shredded LONGHORN CHEESE
1 can (4 oz.) diced GREEN CHILES
1/4 cup diced ONION
chopped JALAPEÑOS, to taste
SALSA

Heat tortillas on an oven rack until slightly firm. Transfer them to a baking sheet. Sprinkle on all ingredients except the salsa. Place under broiler until cheese is bubbly. Allow to cool for a minute before slicing into pizza wedges. Serve with salsa on the side.

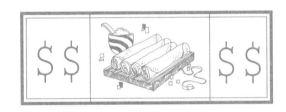

Split a Pair Tortilla Rolls

2 cups grated CHEDDAR CHEESE
1 can (4 oz.) diced GREEN CHILES, drained
3 GREEN ONIONS, chopped (use tops too!)
1 pkg. (8 oz.) CREAM CHEESE, softened
8 oz. SOUR CREAM
6 lg. FLOUR TORTILLAS

Combine first five ingredients. Spread mixture evenly on flat tortilla. Roll up, wrap in plastic wrap, and refrigerate at least 2 hours. Slice at an angle into bite-sized pieces. Serve with your favorite dip.

Spinach Quesadillas

1 pkg. (10 oz.) frozen SPINACH
1/4 cup diced ONION
1/4 cup sharp CHEDDAR CHEESE, grated
6 flour TORTILLAS, 10-12 inch size
BUTTER or MARGARINE, softened

Cook spinach according to package directions. Drain thoroughly, pressing out any excess water. In a small bowl, combine spinach, onion and cheese. Place spinach mixture on one half of each tortilla and fold. Lightly butter both sides and grill in a hot skillet until golden brown. Serves 4-6.

CRAPS — If you see the dice moving rapidly around the table, you can be sure that there are a lot of sevens being rolled. A "Don't Pass" bet might be in order.

Late Night Nachos

1 large bag TORTILLA CHIPS
1/2 lb. cooked GROUND MEAT
1 cup shredded JACK CHEESE
1 cup shredded CHEDDAR CHEESE
1 can (4 oz.) diced GREEN CHILES
3/4 cup chopped ONION
1 can (15 oz.) REFRIED BEANS
3/4 cup chopped TOMATOES

Spread half of the chips evenly on a baking sheet. Combine meat, cheeses, chiles and onions. Drop teaspoonfuls of refried beans on chips and sprinkle with meat mixture. Repeat for second layer. Bake at 325° until cheese bubbles. Sprinkle tomatoes over top and bake an additional five minutes. Serve with **sour cream, guacamole** or **salsa** on the side.

Crab-Zucchini Cups

3 med. (6-inch) ZUCCHINI
2 cans (7 1/2 oz. ea.) CRAB MEAT, drained and flaked
3 GREEN ONIONS, sliced thin
1 cup MAYONNAISE
2 tsp. LEMON JUICE
1/2 tsp. CURRY POWDER
2 cups grated SWISS CHEESE
1 can (8 oz.) WATER CHESTNUTS, diced
PAPRIKA for garnish

Wash zucchini and slice off ends. Cut into one-inch rounds. Scoop out core leaving about 1/4-inch of pulp and place on baking sheet. Combine crab, onion, mayonnaise, lemon juice and curry powder. Stir in water chestnuts and 1 1/2 cups of cheese. Spoon into zucchini rounds. Sprinkle with remaining cheese and paprika. Bake at 400° for 12 minutes. Makes about 15 "cups".

Jokers Wild Cold Bean Dip

1 pkg. (3 oz.) CREAM CHEESE
1 can (16 oz.) REFRIED BEANS
2 Tbsp. ONION
1 tsp. CHILI PEPPER
1/4 tsp. GARLIC POWDER
1 tsp. SALT

Soften cream cheese. Blend in remaining ingredients. Mix well and chill.

Hot Bean Dip

1 can (16 oz.) REFRIED BEANS
1/2 can (4 oz.) diced GREEN CHILES
1/2 lb. CHEDDAR or JACK CHEESE, grated
1 cup canned TOMATOES, drained
1/4 tsp. ONION POWDER
1/4 tsp. SALT
1/4 tsp. GARLIC POWDER

Mix all ingredients well in a skillet and heat until cheese melts, stirring occasionally. Serve warm.

Sweeten the Pot Chile Dip

1/4 cup OLIVE OIL
1/2 cup diced ONION
1 clove GARLIC, crushed
1 JALAPEÑO, seeded and diced or
   1 can (4 oz.) diced GREEN CHILES, drained
1 sm. can TOMATO PASTE
1 can (28 oz.) TOMATOES drained
1 can (15 oz.) TOMATOES AND GREEN CHILES, drained
1 lb. LONGHORN CHEESE, diced

Sauté onions and garlic in olive oil until lightly browned. Add remaining ingredients, except cheese and simmer until medium thick. Add cheese to mixture and simmer until ropy. Keep warm in mini-crock pot or fondue pot while serving.

Players Paté

3 oz. CREAM CHEESE
1/4 lb. BRAUNSWEIGER
1/4 cup WHIPPING CREAM
1/4 tsp. NUTMEG
1/4 cup diced MUSHROOMS

Combine all ingredients in medium bowl. Let stand at room temperature for at least 1/2 hour before serving. Serve with your favorite crackers.

Green Chile Meatballs

1 lg. ONION, minced
OIL
2 lbs. lean GROUND BEEF
1 cup dried BREAD CRUMBS
2 EGGS
1/2 tsp. CHILI POWDER
2 tsp. SEASONED SALT
1/2 tsp. BLACK PEPPER
1 can (8 oz.) diced GREEN CHILES, drained

Sauté onions in oil. In a large bowl, combine meat, bread crumbs, eggs, spices and chiles. Add sautéed onions. Shape meat into 1-inch balls and place on baking pan. Bake at 350 degrees for 15 minutes. Drain grease and return pans to oven for another 15 minutes. Serve on toothpicks garnished with parsley.

Banco Rumaki

1/4 tsp. GARLIC POWDER
1/4 tsp. ground GINGER
1/4 cup DRY SHERRY
1/4 cup SOY SAUCE
2 Tbsp. OIL
1 Tbsp. SUGAR
1/4 cup WATER
12 to 14 CHICKEN LIVERS halved
1 can (8 oz.) sliced WATER CHESTNUTS
12 slices BACON, cut in half

Combine first 7 ingredients in a medium size bowl. Add livers and water chestnuts. Cover and chill for 4 to 6 hours.

Fry bacon lightly (not crisp) and drain. Drain liquid from liver and chestnut mixture. Wrap a piece of bacon around a liver half and a slice of water chestnut. Secure with a wooden toothpick. Broil about 4" from heat for 6 to 8 minutes (turning once).

Chicken Wings in Honey Sauce

8 CHICKEN WINGS

Cut off and discard wing tips. Separate wings at joint to make two pieces. Place chicken in a single layer in baking pan and brush with **Honey Sauce.** Bake in a 375° oven for ten minutes, turn and brush again with sauce. Bake for another 10 minutes or until chicken is tender.

Honey Sauce

1/2 cup KETCHUP
1/4 cup finely chopped ONION
1 Tbsp. HONEY

1 Tbsp. VINEGAR
1 clove GARLIC, minced

Combine all ingredients thoroughly.

Betting at the Roulette Table

Column Bet—A bet on any one of the three columns on the layout, each of which contains twelve numbers. Winning bets are paid off at 2 to 1.

Combination Bet—A wager covering more than one number or more than one choice on the layout, using a single chip or units of chips.

Corner Bet—An inside combination wager of four numbers at the same time, covered by a single chip.

Dozen Bet—A wager on any of three dozens on the table (1 through 12, 13 through 24, and 25 through 36). This wager pays off at 2 to 1.

High-Low Bet—A wager that the next spin of the wheel will come up with either a high number (19 through 36) or a low number (1 through 18). This wager pays off at even money.

Inside Bet—A wager on any of the numbers 0, 00, 1 through 36, or any combination of these numbers.

Odd-Even Bet—A wager that the next spin of the wheel will come up either even or odd. This wager pays off at even money.

Outside Bet—A bet on any choice or event on the wheel other than bets covered by numbers 0, 00, or 1 through 36.

Red-Black Bet—A wager that the next spin of the wheel will come up with a red or a black number. This wager pays off at even money.

Split Bet—A bet on two numbers at one time, both covered with one chip.

Straight Bet—A single bet on any individual choice, such as a number, a column, or an even-money proposition.

Straight-up Bet—A bet on one particular number, either 0, 00, or 1 through 36, which is paid off at 35 to 1.

Trio Bet—An inside combination bet on three numbers at one time.

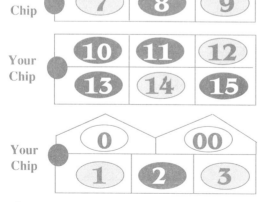

Three Numbers Bet—Also known as a "street", pays 11-1.

Six Numbers Bet—A "double street", pays 5-1.

Five Numbers Bet—One "street" and the 0 and 00 numbers, pays 6-1.

A
♦

Salads & Soups

Strike it Rich Tuna Salad

1 tsp. grated ONION
1 tsp. DRY MUSTARD
1 tsp. SALT
2 Tbsp. chopped PARSLEY
6 Tbsp. LEMON JUICE
1/2 cup SALAD OIL
1/4 cup chopped PIMENTO
1 can (14 oz.) ARTICHOKE HEARTS, drained
2 cans (6 1/2 oz. ea.) chunk TUNA
1/4 lb. MONTEREY JACK, cut into strips
1/2 cup pitted RIPE OLIVES
8 SCALLIONS

Mix first 7 ingredients together in a medium size bowl and add artichoke hearts. Cover and chill several hours. Remove artichokes from marinade with slotted spoon and arrange on platter with tuna chunks, cheese slices, olives and scallions. Serve with reserved marinade. Serves 4.

Stuffed Tomato Salad

6 med. TOMATOES
1 Tbsp. minced ONION
1 Tbsp. chopped GREEN PEPPER
1/2 cup chopped CELERY
1/2 cup chopped CUCUMBER

2 HARD BOILED
   EGGS, chopped
2 Tbsp. MAYONNAISE
1/4 tsp. PEPPER
1 tsp. SALT

Scoop out centers of tomatoes at stem ends leaving shells about 1/4-inch thick. Turn upside down and drain. Dice the tomato pulp and combine with balance of ingredients. Stuff tomatoes with mixture and serve on bed of lettuce leaves. Serves 6.

Bringing Home the Bacon Salad

4 med. TOMATOES, peeled and cut into bite-sized pieces
1/2 cup chopped CELERY
1 med. ONION
2 lg. GREEN PEPPERS, cut into bite-sized pieces
4 slices BACON
1/2 cup VINEGAR
1/2 tsp. SALT
1 tsp. CHILI POWDER
4 HARD BOILED EGGS, sliced
shredded LETTUCE

Fry bacon until crisp, remove from skillet and drain. Combine vegetables and bacon in mixing bowl. Add vinegar, salt and chili powder to bacon fat in skillet and mix well. Pour over vegetables and toss. Serve on a bed of shredded lettuce garnished with egg slices. Serves 4.

Pinto Bean Salad

2 cups cooked PINTO BEANS, drained
3 HARD BOILED EGGS, chopped
2 Tbsp. minced ONION
4 Tbsp. minced PICKLE
1 tsp. PREPARED MUSTARD
1/4 tsp. PEPPER
1/4 cup MAYONNAISE
SALT to taste

Combine all ingredients and serve on a bed of shredded lettuce.

Ace of Spades Potato Salad

4 cups boiled POTATOES, cubed
1/3 cup ITALIAN DRESSING
1 tsp. SALT
1 tsp. instant minced ONION
1 1/2 cups COTTAGE CHEESE
3/4 cup chopped CELERY
1 HARD BOILED EGG, chopped
TOMATO, cut in wedges
LETTUCE

Combine dressing, salt and onion and toss lightly with potatoes. Cover and chill. At serving time, add cottage cheese, celery and egg. Toss lightly again and serve, garnished with tomato wedges on a bed of lettuce.

BLACKJACK — of the 52 cards in a deck, 16 have a value of ten (kings, queens, jacks and tens). Keep this in mind as you play this fascinating game!

Garlic-Chile Salad

3 TOMATOES, chopped
1 lg. can sliced BLACK OLIVES, drained
6 GREEN ONIONS, cut into 1/2 inch pieces
1 can (7 oz.) whole GREEN CHILES, sliced
1 cup GARLIC CROUTONS
4 Tbsp. OLIVE OIL
2 Tbsp. WHITE WINE VINEGAR
LETTUCE

Combine all ingredients (except lettuce) and chill. Serve on bed of lettuce.

Orange Cabbage Slaw

3 med. ORANGES, peeled and cut to bite-sized pieces
1 sm. head CABBAGE, shredded
1/4 cup finely chopped ONION
1 Tbsp. SUGAR
1/2 tsp. SALT
3/4 cup MAYONNAISE
1 Tbsp. LEMON JUICE

Combine oranges, cabbage and onion in large serving bowl. Mix the rest of ingredients and pour over slaw mixture. Toss lightly, cover and refrigerate 20 to 30 minutes before serving.

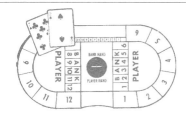

BACCARAT — Named from the French spelling of the Italian word, baccara, meaning zero. In this game all of the tens and face cards have no value!

Banco Lemony Cole Slaw

6 Tbsp. LIGHT CREAM
3 Tbsp. LEMON JUICE
2 1/2 cups chopped CABBAGE
1 1/2 Tbsp. SUGAR
SALT & PEPPER to taste

Combine all ingredients and chill thoroughly before serving. Serves 6.

Twelve Spot Fruit Salad

1/3 cup COCONUT, flaked
1 cup PINEAPPLE CHUNKS
1 cup seedless GRAPES
1 cup miniature MARSHMALLOWS
2 cups peeled and diced ORANGES
2 cups SOUR CREAM
SALT
LETTUCE

   Combine all ingredients. Chill several hours or overnight. Serve on bed of lettuce.

CRAPS — Some casinos pay 3-to-1 for a winning 2 or 12 spot field bet. Keep it in mind if you're feeling lucky!

Casino Country Corn Salad

1 can (15 oz.) whole kernel CORN, drained
1 can (4 oz.) sliced pickled BEETS, drained
1 can (4 oz.) diced GREEN CHILES, drained
6 GREEN ONIONS, cut into 1/2 inch pieces
1/2 cup BELL PEPPER
2 med. TOMATOES, chopped
1/8 tsp. flavored PEPPER, freshly ground
1/4 cup WHITE WINE VINEGAR
1/2 cup OLIVE OIL
LETTUCE

   Combine all ingredients except lettuce in medium bowl. Toss well. Chill until ready to serve. Serve on bed of lettuce leaves.

Garbanzo Bean Salad

1 can (8 3/4 oz.) CORN, drained
1 cup CELERY, diced
2 cups GARBANZOS, cooked, drained
1/2 cup chopped ONION
2 Tbsp. diced PIMENTO
1/4 cup diced GREEN BELL PEPPER

Combine ingredients and toss with salad dressing of choice. Chill before serving.

Fiesta Avocado Salad

1/2 head LETTUCE
1/2 head ROMAINE
1/2 head CHICORY
1/2 pint CHERRY TOMATOES, halved
2 AVOCADOS, peeled and sliced
3 slices BACON, cooked and crumbled
3 oz. ROQUEFORT or BLUE CHEESE, crumbled

Tear greens into bite-sized pieces and place in salad bowl. Add tomatoes and avocados. Sprinkle with bacon and cheese. Toss lightly with *Herb Dressing.*

Herb Dressing

1 cup VEGETABLE OIL
6 Tbsp. WINE VINEGAR
1/4 cup LEMON JUICE
1 tsp. SALT

1 tsp. SUGAR
1/2 tsp. BASIL LEAVES
2 cloves GARLIC, crushed
Dash PEPPER

Combine all ingredients, cover and chill. Makes 1 1/2 cups.

Golden Salad Dressing

2 Tbsp. FLOUR
1 tsp. SALT
1/2 tsp. DRY MUSTARD
1/3 cup SUGAR

2 EGG YOLKS
1/2 cup VINEGAR
1/2 cup WATER
1 Tbsp. BUTTER

Combine dry ingredients. Beat egg yolks in small bowl and add to dry mixture. Heat vinegar, water, and butter in saucepan. Remove from heat and gradually add egg mixture, stirring rapidly. Return to heat, stirring constantly until smooth and thick (about 3 minutes). Makes 1 3/4 cups dressing.

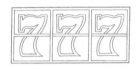

Lucky Seven Dressing

1 cup SOUR CREAM
2 Tbsp. VINEGAR
1 Tbsp. LEMON JUICE
1/2 tsp. SALT

1 Tbsp. minced GREEN
  ONION
3 Tbsp. SUGAR

Blend ingredients and chill. Makes 1 1/4 cups dressing.

Fruit Juice Dressing

3 Tbsp. LEMON JUICE
3 Tbsp. ORANGE JUICE
3-4 Tbsp. SALAD OIL

1/4 tsp. SALT
2 Tbsp. SUGAR

Combine all ingredients thoroughly. Chill until ready to serve. Makes 1 cup dressing.

Three Queens Orange Soup

2 Tbsp. quick-cooking TAPIOCA
2 1/2 cups ORANGE JUICE
2 Tbsp. SUGAR
dash of SALT
2 CINNAMON STICKS
1 1/2 cups ORANGE SECTIONS
1 pkg. (12 oz.) frozen sliced PEACHES
1 BANANA, sliced

Combine tapioca, orange juice, sugar and salt in saucepan. Let stand 5 minutes. Add cinnamon sticks and bring to a boil over medium heat. Remove from heat and cool for 20 minutes. Remove cinnamon sticks, add thawed and diced peaches and banana. Heat and serve. Serves 6 to 8.

Which cards would *you* "hold"?

Chicken-Rice-Lemon Soup

4 cans condensed CHICKEN BROTH
1/4 cup uncooked RICE
2 EGGS, beaten
3 Tbsp. LEMON JUICE
1/2 tsp. grated LEMON PEEL
1 LEMON, sliced very thin

Combine chicken broth and rice. Cover and simmer until rice is tender. Drain chicken broth and reserve 2 cups. Beat eggs and lemon juice together. Pour two cups of hot broth very slowly into egg-lemon mixture. Pour egg mixture into saucepan with rice and add lemon peel. Reheat, but do not boil. Serve with lemon slices floating in each bowl.

Meatball Soup
(Sopa de Albondigas)
Soup

1 ONION, minced
1 clove GARLIC, minced
2 Tbsp. OIL
1/2 can TOMATO SAUCE
3 qts. BEEF STOCK
sprig of MINT in soup, or
 chopped mint leaves in meatballs

Sauté onion and garlic in oil. Add tomato sauce and beef stock and heat to boiling point. Add sprig of mint to broth about 10 minutes before it boils.

Meatballs

3/4 lb. GROUND BEEF
3/4 lb. GROUND PORK
1/3 cup uncooked RICE
1 1/2 tsp. SALT
1/4 tsp. PEPPER
1 EGG, slightly beaten

Mix meat with rice, salt and pepper, egg and mint leaves. Shape into small balls. Drop into boiling soup. Cover tightly and cook about 1/2 hour.

VIDEO POKER — If your first cards are a winner (flush, straight, four of a kind etc.) be sure to push the hold button on *all* of the cards you want to keep. Do not push the draw/deal button first or you'll lose your winning hand.

Green Chile Soup

1 Tbsp. cooking OIL
1 ONION, chopped
1 can (7 oz.) diced GREEN CHILES
1 can (7 oz.) TOMATO SAUCE
6 to 7 cups WATER
SALT
1 POTATO, diced
2 cloves GARLIC, minced
1/2 lb. LONGHORN CHEESE, grated

Sauté onion lightly in cooking oil. Add chiles and tomato sauce and cook for 10 minutes. Add water, salt, potatoes and garlic. Simmer until potatoes are done. Add cheese, stir and serve. Serves 6 to 8

Break the Bank Beef Minestrone

1 clove GARLIC
1/2 cup sliced CELERY
1 ZUCCHINI, sliced
1 cup shredded CABBAGE
2 Tbsp. OLIVE OIL
1 pkg. frozen cooked MIXED VEGETABLES
1 can (15 oz.) KIDNEY, PINTO or GARBANZO BEANS
1 can (16 oz.) TOMATOES
1 can (16 oz.) BEEF BROTH
1 cup cooked BEEF, cubed
2 cups cooked PASTA
SALT, PEPPER and OREGANO

Sauté garlic, celery, zucchini and cabbage in olive oil. In a large saucepan, combine vegetables with beans, tomatoes, broth, beef and pasta. Heat thoroughly. Add salt, pepper and oregano to taste. Serves 6 to 8.

Go for the Gold Garbanzo Soup

2 Tbsp. OIL
1/2 cup diced CELERY
1/2 cup diced ONIONS
1/2 cup diced GREEN BELL PEPPER
1 clove GARLIC
1/4 tsp. CHILI POWDER
1/4 tsp. OREGANO
1 Tbsp. fresh CILANTRO
5 cups WATER
1 Tbsp. powdered CHICKEN BOUILLON
1/4 cup uncooked RICE
1 Tbsp. chopped PIMENTOS
1/2 cup GREEN CHILE SALSA
1/2 cup GARBANZO BEANS
1 1/2 tsp. CORNSTARCH
1 AVOCADO, diced

Sauté celery, onions, pepper and garlic in oil. Add chili powder, oregano, cilantro and cook for 2 minutes. Add water and let come to a boil. Add next five ingredients. Cook for 25 minutes at low simmer. Thicken soup with cornstarch dissolved in cool water. Simmer 5 minutes more. Serve, garnishing each bowl with diced avocado.

Serves 8.

BACCARAT — In this game if the cards dealt to you add up to 8 or 9 you have a winning hand (a "natural"). If the total points of your cards add up to 10 or more, only the last digit is counted. For instance: two fives (10 points) = 0. A five and a seven (12 points) = 2. Tens and face cards = 0.

Gazpacho with Avocado

1 can (16 oz.) whole peeled TOMATOES
1 med. GREEN PEPPER, chopped
1 med. AVOCADO, cubed
1/2 CUCUMBER, sliced
1 can (2 oz.) PIMENTOS, drained and chopped
2 Tbsp. SALAD OIL
2 Tbsp. WINE VINEGAR
1 tsp. SALT
1 tsp. SUGAR
1/2 cup CROUTONS

Reserving the juice from the can of tomatoes, cut tomatoes into bite-sized pieces. Combine with the rest of the ingredients (except croutons). Cover and chill until serving time. Pour into small soup bowls and garnish with croutons.

Progressive Pinto Bean Soup

3 cups dry PINTO BEANS
2 HAM HOCKS or 2 slices HAM
1 cup diced ONIONS
1 cup diced CELERY
1 can (8 oz.) TOMATO SAUCE
1 can (10 1/2 oz.) TOMATO SOUP
SALT, PEPPER and VEGETABLE SALT, to taste

In a large pot, cover beans with water and add ham hocks or ham (diced). When almost done, add onions, celery, tomato sauce and soup. Add salt, pepper and vegetable salt to taste. Add water as needed to desired thickness.

Gambler's Stew

1 1/2 lbs. lean STEW BEEF
1 ONION, chopped
1 clove GARLIC, chopped
1/4 cup OIL
1/2 cup TOMATO SAUCE
1 cup WATER
3 Tbsp. WINE VINEGAR
1 tsp. SALT
1/2 tsp. PEPPER
1/2 tsp. OREGANO
3 lg. CARROTS, cut into bite-sized pieces
3 lg. POTATOES, cut into bite-sized pieces

Put all ingredients (except carrots and potatoes) into 2-quart saucepan. Cover and simmer over low heat for 1 1/2-2 hours. Add the vegetables and continue simmering until meat is tender. Serves 4 to 6.

Barbecue Grill Stew

1 lb. STEW MEAT, cut into bite-sized pieces
4 sm. whole WHITE ONIONS
4 CARROTS, thinly sliced
4 POTATOES, cut into bite-sized chunks
CELERY SALT, GARLIC SALT, SALT & PEPPER
1 cup WATER
1 pkg. (1 1/4 oz.) BEEF GRAVY MIX

Divide meat and vegetables into four servings. Place on individual pieces of foil. Add seasonings to taste. Combine water and gravy mix. Pour about 1/4 cup gravy over each serving. Fold foil over (double at seam), and cook about half an hour, turning twice.

Meatball Stew

1 lb. GROUND CHUCK
1 ONION, chopped
4 POTATOES, sliced small
4 ONIONS, quartered

Combine hamburger and onion and roll into small meat balls. Place in skillet or pan. Add vegetables, soup and water. Mix all together and simmer until potatoes are done. Serves 4.

BLACKJACK — Want to look like a high roller? Instead of saying "hit me", scrape your cards towards yourself on the table or nod your head and tap on your cards when its your turn.

Easy Chili Con Carne

1 1/2 cups dry PINTO BEANS
1/2 cup diced SALT PORK
1/2 cup chopped ONION
1 clove GARLIC, minced
1/2 lb. lean GROUND BEEF or PORK
2 to 4 tsp. CHILE POWDER
1 can (28 oz.) crushed TOMATOES
SALT and PEPPER to taste

Soak pinto beans overnight covered in water. Rinse beans thoroughly, place in a large saucepan and cover with water. Cook until tender. Fry the salt pork until crisp, set aside. Brown the onion and garlic in the pork fat. Add meat, stir, and cook slowly for five minutes. Add chili powder and tomatoes. Combine meat mixture and salt pork with beans. Add salt and pepper to taste and simmer until meat is tender. Serves 6 to 8.

Hot, Hot, Hot Chili!

1 lg. ONION, chopped
2 Tbsp. OIL
2 lbs. lean GROUND BEEF
1 can (16 oz.) TOMATOES
2 cans (8 oz. ea.) TOMATO SAUCE
1 tsp. SUGAR
2 tsp. ground CUMIN
2 tsp. PAPRIKA
2 lg. cloves GARLIC, crushed
1 can BEER
2 fresh JALAPEÑO PEPPERS, minced fine
5 Tbsp. CHILI POWDER
SALT and CAYENNE PEPPER to taste

Sauté onion in oil. Add chili meat, stir and cook until no longer pink. Add remaining ingredients and cook until thick (about 1 1/2 hours). Serves 4 to 6.

Not Quite So Hot Chili

2 lg. ONIONS, chopped
2 lbs. GROUND BEEF
1 lb. GROUND PORK
1 lb. GROUND CHICKEN BREAST
2 GREEN CHILE PEPPERS, seeded and chopped
1/2 cup chopped CELERY
2 cloves GARLIC, mashed
2 pkgs. LAWRY'S® CHILI MIX
1 can (28 oz.) stewed TOMATOES
1 Tbsp. SALT

Sauté onions in a small amount of oil. Add beef, pork, and chicken and cook for about one-half hour, stirring often. Add peppers, celery and garlic and continue stirring. Add chili mix, tomatoes and salt and cook slowly for two or three hours. Add water to desired thickness.   Makes about 1 gallon of medium hot chili.

Can't Lose Chili Con Carne

1 lb. cubed ROUND STEAK or 2 lbs. GROUND BEEF
SALT, PEPPER and GARLIC SALT
2 Tbsp. MARGARINE
1 cup CELERY, with leaves
3 cans (16 oz. ea.) TOMATOES
2 cans (6 oz.) TOMATO PASTE
2 Tbsp. SUGAR
1 can (15 oz.) PINTO BEANS
1 Tbsp. WORCESTERSHIRE SAUCE
Dash of OREGANO
1/2 cup PARSLEY
1 can RIPE OLIVES, pitted and quartered
Additional seasonings:
  2-4 Tbsp. CHILI POWDER
  CAYENNE PEPPER
  TABASCO® SAUCE
  BAY LEAF
  GREEN BELL PEPPER, diced
  1/2 cup ONION, chopped

    Coat beef with salt, pepper and garlic salt. Sauté beef and
celery in margarine. Cover and simmer for 10 minutes stirring
occasionally. Add next 7 ingredients and simmer 5-10 minutes.
Add remaining seasonings to taste. Serves 4 to 6.

BLACKJACK — Blackjack is by far the most popular casino game in the United States, with more players generating more casino revenue than craps, roulette, and baccarat combined.

At the Craps Table

A glossary of craps terms

Any craps—A wager on the craps table where the player may bet that the next roll of the dice will come up 2, 3, or 12.

Any Seven—A wager on the craps table where the player may bet that the next throw of the dice will come up 7.

Back line—A wager on either the don't pass or don't come.

Big Six and Big Eight—A wager on the craps table where the player bets that either a 6 or 8, or both, will be thrown before a 7 is rolled.

Boxman—The casino executive in charge of a particular craps table.

Come Bet—A wager that can only be placed after the come out roll. If the shooter's next roll is 7 or 11 the player wins. If the shooter rolls a 2, 3, or 12 the player loses. If the shooter produces a point, it becomes the come bettor's point and his wager is moved to that box. If the shooter makes his point the player wins. If the shooter rolls a 7 the player loses.

Come-out Roll—Any roll made before a point is established.

Craps/Crapping Out—**1.** The name of the game. **2.** Rolling a 2, 3, or 12.

Don't-come—A wager made after the come-out roll against the dice passing.

Don't-pass—A wager that the shooter will crap out on the come-out roll.

Easy Way—The roll of a 4, 6, 8, or 10 other than as a pair. An "easy" 4 is a throw of the dice showing a 1 and a 3.

Field Bet—A one-roll wager placed in the Field box bets that the next roll of the dice will be either a 2, 3, 4, 9, 10, 11, 12.

Hardway Bet—A wager placed in hardway boxes indicating a pair of dice (2's, 3's, 4's, or 5's). To win, the dice must come up in the exact pair of the player's wager before that total is thrown as an "easy" number (4, 6, 8, 10), or before a 7 is thrown. Payoffs are shown in each of the boxes.

Marker Puck/Buck—A black and white marker that the dealer places white side up on the numbered box indicating the shooters point.

Pass—A wager made that the shooter will either roll a natural 7 or 11 on the first roll (come out), or will roll his "point" (and win) before rolling a 7.

Place Bets—Numbered boxes on the playing table showing 4, 5, 6, 8, 9, and 10. A wager in one of these boxes bets that those numbers will be thrown (whether in pairs or not) before a 7 is thrown.

Point—Numbers 4, 5, 6, 8, 9, and 10 thrown on the come-out roll become the shooter's point and must be repeated before a 7 is thrown to win.

Roll—A single throw of the dice. Also, a complete cycle or series of throws of the dice until the shooter throws a 7 and loses.

K
♠

Breads

Cornmeal-Cheddar Cheese Bread

1 1/2 cups CHEDDAR CHEESE, grated
1/2 cup BACON, fried crisp and crumbled
1 cup MILK
2 Tbsp. BUTTER
4 EGG YOLKS, beaten (reserve the whites)
1 cup YELLOW CORNMEAL
1/2 cup FLOUR
1 tsp. SALT
1 Tbsp. BAKING POWDER

Mix first five ingredients together and set aside. Combine dry ingredients and then mix with the cheese mixture until just moist. Fold in egg whites that have been beaten until they form peaks. Pour into greased baking dish and bake at 400° for 30 minutes.

BLACKJACK — Double down on 10 or 11 points only if the dealer's hand is showing two through nine.

Double Down Pumpkin Bread

3 1/3 cups all-purpose
   FLOUR, sifted
2 tsp. BAKING SODA
1 1/2 tsp. SALT
1 tsp. CINNAMON
1 tsp. NUTMEG

4 EGGS
2/3 cup WATER
3 cups SUGAR
1 can (16 oz.) PUMPKIN
1 cup OIL
1 cup chopped NUTS

Combine flour, baking soda, salt, cinnamon and nutmeg in a large bowl and mix well. In another bowl, beat eggs well, add sugar, pumpkin and oil and mix thoroughly. Combine mixtures and pour into two loaf pans. Bake in 350° oven for 1 hour.

Pecan Coffeecake with Pecan Topping

Sift together:

3 cups sifted FLOUR
3 tsp. BAKING POWDER
1 tsp. SALT
1/4 tsp. NUTMEG
1 tsp. CINNAMON
1 cup SUGAR

Blend in:

1/4 cup BUTTER
2 EGGS, unbeaten
1 cup MILK

Stir mixture until smooth.

Add:

1/4 cup chopped PECANS

Pour mixture into a well-greased, round cake pan. Spread *Pecan Topping* over top, sprinkle with 1/2 cup pecans, and bake at 375° for 25 minutes. When cake has cooled, split into two layers and spread **1/2 cup whipped HEAVY CREAM,** on bottom half. Replace top layer, cut and serve.

Pecan Topping

1/4 cup BUTTER	**1 tsp. CINNAMON**
1 cup BROWN SUGAR	**1/8 tsp. SALT**
3 Tbsp. FLOUR	**1/2 cup chopped PECANS**

In a medium-sized bowl, cream together the butter, brown sugar and flour. Add cinnamon and salt and stir. Reserve pecans.

Royal Bran Muffins

1/4 cup HONEY
1/4 cup SHORTENING or BUTTER, softened
1 EGG
3/4 cup MILK
1 cup WHOLE BRAN
1 cup pitted and diced DATES
1 cup all-purpose FLOUR
2 tsp. BAKING POWDER
1/2 tsp. SALT

Cream together shortening and honey. Add egg and beat well. Stir in milk, bran and dates. Sift together dry ingredients. Add to date mixture. Stir just to moisten ingredients. Fill greased muffin tins 2/3 full. Bake in preheated oven at 400° for 20 minutes. Makes 1 dozen muffins.

Golden Honey Muffins

2 cups all-purpose FLOUR
1 tsp. SALT
3 tsp. BAKING POWDER
1 cup MILK

4 Tbsp. HONEY
1 EGG, beaten
1/4 cup SHORTENING, melted

Sift flour with salt and baking powder. Combine milk, honey, egg, and melted shortening. Add to flour mixture. Stir quickly, long enough to just moisten ingredients. Fill greased muffin tins one-half full. Bake at 400° for 25 to 30 minutes or until golden brown. Makes 1 dozen muffins. Serve with *Orange Honey Butter.*

Orange Honey Butter

1/2 cup (1 stick) BUTTER
2 Tbsp. HONEY
2 Tbsp. frozen concentrated ORANGE JUICE

In a small bowl, cream butter until softened. Gradually add honey and beat until light and fluffy. Continue beating while slowly adding orange juice.

Bingo Biscuits

2 cups FLOUR
1 Tbsp. BAKING POWDER
1/2 tsp. SUGAR
1/2 tsp. SALT
1/4 cup SHORTENING
2/3 cup MILK

Sift dry ingredients together. Cut in shortening until mixture is the size of coarse salt. Add milk. Roll out to 1/2-inch thickness on floured surface. Cut with floured cutter and place on ungreased baking sheet. Bake in preheated oven at 450° for about 12 minutes.

CRAPS — Often considered one of the best bets in the house, put your money on the Pass Line if you like the looks of the player with the dice or, more importantly, if he's winning.

Buttermilk Biscuits

2 cups FLOUR
1 tsp. SALT
1/2 tsp. BAKING SODA

1 tsp. BAKING POWDER
3 Tbsp. BUTTER
1 cup BUTTERMILK

Combine flour, salt, baking soda and baking powder. Cut in butter until mixture is coarse in texture. Gradually stir in buttermilk, adding only enough to make a soft dough. On floured surface, roll dough out to 1/2-inch thickness. Cut with floured cutter and place on ungreased baking sheet. Bake in preheated oven at 400° for about 12 minutes.

Scones

2 cups all-purpose FLOUR
1 Tbsp. SUGAR
1 Tbsp. BAKING POWDER
1/2 tsp. SALT
1/4 cup BUTTER
1/3 cup MILK
2 EGGS
Variation: add 6 Tbsp. any DRIED FRUIT

Sift flour. Sift flour again with sugar, baking powder and salt. Cut butter into dry ingredients. Beat milk and eggs together and stir into dry ingredients blending thoroughly. Knead half a dozen times on floured board. Roll out to 4-inch squares, 1/2 -inch thick and cut each square into two triangles. Preheat frying pan (no grease) and place scones on surface. Heat on each side for 10 minutes.

Makes 6 to 8 scones.

Corn Popovers

1 can (15 oz.) CORN KERNELS
1/4 cup MILK
2 EGGS
1 cup FLOUR
1/4 tsp. BAKING POWDER
1 tsp. SUGAR
1/2 tsp. SALT
1/2 tsp. WHITE PEPPER
1/4 tsp. CAYENNE
1/4 tsp. CRUSHED RED
    PEPPER
1 med. JALAPEÑO

Purée corn with milk in blender. Remove from blender and strain. Return juice to blender and add remaining ingredients. Blend until completely smooth. Let batter rest about 1 hour. Grease popover pans thoroughly and place in preheated 450° over for 2 minutes before adding batter. Fill pans to 2/3 full and bake 15 minutes. Reduce heat to 375° and bake 10 to 15 minutes more or until light brown.

Double Bar
Banana-Orange Bread

2 1/2 cups all-purpose
    FLOUR, sifted
4 tsp. BAKING POWDER
3/4 tsp. SALT
3/4 cup chopped NUTS
1 1/2 cups MIXED CANDIED
    FRUITS

1/3 cup RAISINS
1/2 cup SHORTENING
3/4 cup SUGAR
3 EGGS
1/2 cup mashed BANANA
1/2 cup ORANGE JUICE

Sift together flour, baking powder and salt. Stir in nuts, candied fruits and raisins. In a separate bowl, cream shortening, add sugar and beat until light and fluffy. Add eggs, one at a time, beating after each addition. Combine mashed banana and orange juice; add to creamed mixture. Stir in flour mixture a little at a time until all is incorporated. Turn into a greased 9 x 5 x 3 loaf pan. Bake for 1 1/4 hours at 350°. Cool at least one-half hour before removing from pan.

Jacks or Better Date-Nut Bread

1 1/2 cups diced DATES
1 1/2 cups boiling WATER
2 Tbsp. BUTTER
2 3/4 cups FLOUR, sifted
1 cup SUGAR

1 tsp. BAKING SODA
1/2 tsp. SALT
1 EGG
1 cup chopped NUTS

Cover dates with boiling water. Add the butter and let stand at room temperature. Sift dry ingredients. Add to date mixture and mix. Add egg, mix well and add nuts. Bake in loaf pan at 325° for one hour and 15 minutes.

Baccarat is for Everybody!

Far from being a celebrity-only complex game, baccarat is as simple as ABC and you can learn to play it in just a few minutes!

A glossary of American baccarat terms

Active player—The player to whom the cards are dealt by the holder of the shoe or the banker. This player represents all the players at the table in American baccarat.

American baccarat—The version of baccarat played in American and Caribbean casinos. The casino books all bets, whether made on the Bank or Player hand. There are no rule options.

Baccarat—The name of the game (a French spelling of an Italian word) pronounced bah-cah-ráh. Also a term in the game meaning a hand with zero points.

Bank; Bank hand—The opponent of the Player hand. This hand receives the cards last, acts last, and must have a higher total than the Player hand in order to win that round of play.

Burned cards—Cards removed from the shoe and dealt out to the discard slot prior to play.

Caller, callman—The dealer who runs the game of baccarat.

Commission—The amount, usually 5 percent, that the casino charges on all winning Bank-hand bets.

Dealer—The house employee who services the game.

Draw a card—The taking of a third card to a hand, either forced by the rules of play or at the option of the player.

Face cards—Jacks, queens, and kings, all of which are valued at zero in baccarat.

Ladderman—A casino executive who supervises the game from a vantage point above the table.

Natural—The term used to describe the total of 8 or 9 dealt as the original two cards.

Player; Player hand—The hand in opposition to the Bank hand. Player hand receives cards first and acts upon them first.

Rules Card—The card that contains all the rules for the game. These rules must be followed by the participants in the game.

Shoe—The box used to deal out cards in baccarat. Shoes hold from three to eight decks of cards.

Tie bet—A wager that the next round of play will produce a tie between the Bank and Player hands.

Main Dishes

Blackjack Beef Burritos

1 can (15 oz.) TOMATOES
1/2 tsp. GARLIC POWDER
3 GREEN ONIONS, chopped
1 can (4 oz.) diced GREEN CHILES
1 lb. cooked, shredded ROAST BEEF
1 can (16 oz.) REFRIED BEANS
1 pkg. (10-12) burrito size FLOUR TORTILLAS

Combine first 5 ingredients in a large saucepan and cook slowly for 30 minutes. Add refried beans, mix well and cook 15 minutes longer. In a skillet over medium heat warm each tortilla briefly. Spread 1/4 cup of bean mixture on each tortilla. Fold tortillas toward the center on two sides so that the bottom forms a "v" shape. Roll up from the bottom and place seam side down on serving plate. Serve with sour cream and salsa on the side.

BLACKJACK — A good rule of thumb is to always play as if the dealer's face down card is a 10.

Chicken Fried Steak

1 lb. ROUND STEAK, cut into
   serving pieces
SEASONED FLOUR*

1 EGG, beaten
2 Tbsp. WATER
1/2 cup OIL

*Combine 1/2 cup flour and 1/2 tsp. each; salt, paprika and pepper. Add water to the beaten egg and mix well. Dredge steak pieces in seasoned flour, dip in egg mixture and dredge again in seasoned flour. Brown steak on both sides in hot oil in skillet. Cover and cook slowly 20 to 30 minutes.

Gringo Tamale Pie

1 ONION, shredded
1 clove GARLIC
1/2 cup OLIVE OIL
1 GREEN BELL PEPPER, diced
1 lb ground ROUND STEAK
1/4 lb. ground PORK
1 can (16 oz.) TOMATOES
1/2 cup diced BLACK OLIVES
1 can (4 oz.) diced GREEN CHILES
SALT, PEPPER & CAYENNE, to taste
1 cup CHEESE, grated
1 tsp. CHILI POWDER
2 Tbsp. CORNMEAL
1 cup CORNMEAL
3 cups WATER

Sauté onion and garlic in oil. Add green peppers, steak and pork to onion mixture. Add tomatoes, olives peppers and seasonings and cook very slowly for one hour. Add grated cheese, chili powder and two tablespoons cornmeal. Stir in well and cook for a few minutes longer.

Mix 1 cup of cornmeal with 3 cups of water. Pour meat mixture into a shallow baking dish and cover with the cornmeal mixture. Bake uncovered in 375° oven for 30 minutes. Garnish with additional olives.

Baked Empañadas
(Turnovers)

3 cups FLOUR
2 tsp. BAKING POWDER
1/2 tsp. SALT

1/2 cup SHORTENING
3 Tbsp. SUGAR
1/2 cup MILK

Sift the dry ingredients together. Cut in shortening. Add milk to hold dough together and beat. Roll on lightly floured board to 1/8-inch thickness and cut out circles with floured cutter (about 12 circles).

Fill with chili, taco meat or fruit mixtures—about 2 tablespoons each. Moisten dough edges with cold water and fold in half. Seal edges by pinching. Bake at 350° for 20 to 30 minutes. Sprinkle fruit empañadas with confectioners sugar. Top meat and chili empañadas with salsa or other favorite toppings.

Chimichangas à la Casino

1 lb. ground ROUND STEAK
1 can (15 oz.) BLACK BEANS, drained
2 cans (4 oz. ea.) diced GREEN CHILES, undrained
1/4 cup sliced GREEN ONIONS
1 can (4 oz.) sliced BLACK OLIVES, drained
LETTUCE
grated CHEESE
SALSA

Fry ground steak in skillet until no longer pink and set aside. Add beans, chiles, onions and olives to skillet. Sauté lightly. Add beef and stir well. Spoon equal amounts of beef mixture onto each tortilla. Fold tortillas, envelope style, and place seam side down on baking sheet. Bake in 400° oven for 30 minutes. Garnish with lettuce, cheese and salsa.

Serves 4.

Big Winner Carne Asada

2 lbs. TOP SIRLOIN, cut into 4 serving-size portions
1/2 tsp. dried CILANTRO
1/4 tsp. ground CUMIN
1/4 tsp. ground ALLSPICE
2 Tbsp. LIME JUICE
2 can (4 oz. ea.) diced GREEN CHILES, undrained

Place steak in crockpot. Combine all other ingredients and spread evenly over steak. Cook for 8 to 10 hours on low setting.

BAR	BAR	BAR

Chili Pot Roast with Gravy

2 Tbsp. FLOUR	2 med. ONIONS
1 tsp. CHILI POWDER	16 cloves GARLIC
1 Tbsp. PAPRIKA	1/3 cup WATER
2 tsp. SALT	1 CINNAMON STICK
4 to 5 lb. POT ROAST	2 Tbsp. FLOUR
3 Tbsp. OIL	1/4 cup WATER

Combine flour, chili powder, paprika and salt. Dredge pot roast in seasoned flour. In heavy skillet, brown roast in oil. Drain oil and add onions, garlic, water and cinnamon stick. Cover and cook slowly for 2 1/2 to 3 hours or until tender.

Remove meat to hot platter. To make gravy, remove cinnamon stick and measure remaining cooking liquid. Add enough water to make two cups. Mix flour with 1/4 cup water and add to pan. Cook, stirring constantly, until thickened. Serve roast sliced with potatoes or rice and with gravy on the side. Serves 6 to 8.

Let it Ride Lamb Chops

4 LAMB CHOPS
2 1/2 tsp. dried ROSEMARY
2 1/2 tsp. GARLIC POWDER
1 cups medium dry WHITE WINE

Place chops in single layer in baking pan. Combine garlic and rosemary and sprinkle equally over chops. Pour wine in pan. Bake at 375° until done to taste. Medium-well takes about 45 minutes.

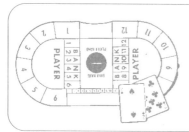

BACCARAT — Regardless of how many people are playing, only two hands are dealt. One is designated the Banker's hand and the other is the Player's hand.

Terrific Teriyaki Beef

2 lbs. FLANK STEAK
1 cup SOY SAUCE
3 Tbsp. SALAD OIL

1 clove GARLIC, sliced
1/4 tsp. GINGER

Combine soy sauce, oil, garlic and ginger and marinate flanks in refrigerator for at least 30 minutes (all day is better).

Broil in moderate, preheated broiler 3 to 5 minutes on each side, basting with reserved marinade. Slice into very thin strips diagonally across grain. Serve with topping of juices from broiler pan.

Cash in Chicken Limón

3 lbs. FRYING CHICKEN, cut into serving pieces.
GARLIC POWDER or GARLIC SALT
1 tsp. crushed OREGANO
1 tsp. grated LEMON PEEL
1/4 cup LEMON JUICE
1/4 cup WATER

Sprinkle chicken with garlic powder (or salt). Place in shallow baking pan, skin-side-down. Combine balance of ingredients and pour over chicken. Bake uncovered at 400° for 15 minutes. Turn chicken. Continue to bake (about 40 minutes, or until tender) basting with pan drippings occasionally. Drippings may be used over chicken, or on side dishes such as rice or noodles.

KENO — Rules vary as to when you must cash in your winning tickets. Be sure and check with your casino, or you may lose, even if you win!

Chile Pork Chops

4 PORK CHOPS
2 LEMONS, peeled and sliced
1 ONION, sliced
1 can (4 oz.) diced GREEN CHILES
1 tsp. SALT
1 1/2 cups TOMATO JUICE
3/4 Tbsp. BUTTER (per chop)

Place chops in large baking pan. Cover with lemon, onion and chile. Sprinkle with salt and add tomato juice. Add butter to tops of each chop. Cover tightly and cook for 1 1/2 hours. Serves 2.

Marinated Steak Kabobs

1/2 cup SOY SAUCE
1/2 tsp. GINGER
2 Tbsp. SALAD OIL
1 Tbsp. SUGAR
2 lbs. boneless STEAK, cut to 1-inch cubes
1 cup PINEAPPLE CHUNKS, drained
CHERRY TOMATOES

Combine soy sauce, ginger, salad oil and sugar. Place meat in a shallow pan and cover with soy sauce marinade. Let stand at least 1 hour turning occasionally.

Place meat on skewers, leaving about 1/4-inch between pieces. Broil meat over hot coals. Place pineapple chunks and tomatoes on separate skewers and cook about half as long as the meat. Brush both with remaining marinade while cooking.

U Win Ham Croquettes

1/2 cup crushed fine BREAD CRUMBS
1 Tbsp. PARSLEY
1 Tbsp. MUSTARD
1/4 cup chopped ONION
1 EGG beaten lightly
1 1/2 cups GROUND HAM, cooked

Combine dry ingredients. Add egg and onion and mix well. Fold in ham. Shape into 3" logs and dust with more bread crumbs. Fry one minute or until golden brown on all sides. Drain on paper towels before serving. Serves 4.

Honey Glazed Chicken Wings

1/2 cup HONEY
3 Tbsp. CORNSTARCH
1/2 tsp. GINGER
1 tsp. SALT
1/4 tsp. PEPPER

3/4 cup COLD WATER
1/3 cup LEMON JUICE
1/4 cup SOY SAUCE
3 lbs. CHICKEN WINGS

Combine all ingredients (except wings) in saucepan in order listed, stirring to make smooth. Heat, stirring constantly, until mixture thickens and comes to a boil. Boil three minutes.

Clip off tips of wings and place in single layer in baking pan and bake at 400° for 10 minutes. Brush glaze over wings and continue baking, turning and glazing until wings are tender.

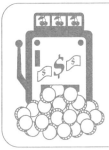

SLOT MACHINES — Some machines are not set to pay out the full amount of big winnings. *Stay with your machine* until the attendant comes over and DO NOT insert any more coins.

Full-pay Broiled Fish

3/4 tsp. PAPRIKA
1 1/2 tsp. SALT
1/4 cup OIL
1/4 cup LEMON JUICE
2 lbs. FISH (halibut, turbot, sea bass etc.)

Combine oil and seasonings. Place fish on well-greased broiler pan and brush inside and out with seasoned oil. Broil about 4 inches from heat for five to eight minutes. Turn fish carefully and brush on remaining oil. Again, broil for five to eight minutes or until fish flakes easily. Serves 4.

Red Wine Lasagna

1 lb. GROUND BEEF
1 can (16 oz.) TOMATOES
1 can (8 oz.) TOMATO SAUCE
1 cup RED WINE
1/2 cup chopped ONION
1 clove GARLIC, minced
3 Tbsp. FLOUR
1 1/4 tsp. SALT
1/2 tsp. SUGAR
1/4 tsp. PEPPER
1/2 tsp. dried OREGANO LEAVES
1/2 tsp. dried BASIL
2 cups CREAMED COTTAGE CHEESE
1 EGG, beaten
1/4 cup PARSLEY, chopped
6 oz. LASAGNA NOODLES, cooked

Stir and cook beef in large skillet over medium heat until no longer pink. Add tomatoes, tomato sauce, wine, onion and garlic and blend in flour. Bring to a boil and then simmer, uncovered, 10 minutes. Add 1 teaspoon of salt, sugar, 1/8 teaspoon of pepper, sage and cinnamon. Cook until mixture thickens and comes to a boil. Remove from heat.

Mix cottage cheese, egg, parsley, 1/4 teaspoon salt and 1/8 teaspoon pepper in a bowl.

In 11 x 7 baking dish, layer half of noodles and spoon half of cottage cheese mixture over noodles. Layer half of meat mixture next, then repeat with remaining lasagna noodles, cheese and meat mixtures. Bake uncovered at 350° for 30 minutes.

Serves 6.

Barbecued Spareribs

4 to 6 lbs. LEAN SPARERIBS
1/2 cup MAPLE SYRUP
1/2 cup CATSUP
1/8 tsp. VINEGAR
1 Tbsp. WORCESTERSHIRE SAUCE
2 tsp. ONION SALT
1/2 tsp. CHILI POWDER
1 tsp. DRY MUSTARD

Cut spareribs into two-rib sections. Blend remaining ingredients. Brush the curved side of ribs with sauce. Arrange in single layer, sauce side down, in shallow baking pan. Brush top of ribs with sauce. Cover with aluminum foil and bake at 375° for 45 minutes. Uncover and continue baking about 1 hour more, or until tender. Brush four or five times with remaining sauce during baking. Serves 4.

POKER — A poker hand with all five cards of the same suit (hearts, diamonds, clubs, spades) is called a **flush.**

Spade Flush Glazed Ribs

4 Tbsp. SOY SAUCE
1/4 tsp. freshly-ground BLACK PEPPER
3 drops TABASCO® SAUCE
1 1/2 cups HONEY
3 lbs. SPARE RIBS

Combine first three ingredients and baste ribs. Pour half of the honey over all and let stand for one-half hour. Turn ribs, baste thoroughly with sauce and cover with remaining honey. Let stand for another half-hour. Roast at 350° for about an hour and a half. Turn and baste occasionally while baking. Serves 4.

Beat the Dealer Tuna Loaf

2 EGGS
1/2 cup MILK
2 cups SOFT BREAD CRUMBS
1/4 cup minced ONION, minced
1 Tbsp. PARSLEY FLAKES
1/4 tsp. THYME
1 tsp. SALT
1/4 tsp. PEPPER
3 cans (6 oz. ea.) TUNA

Combine eggs, milk, bread crumbs and seasonings in mixing bowl. Blend together. Add tuna and mix thoroughly. Put into foil-lined loaf pan. Bake at 375° for one hour. Serve, topped with *Parsley Sauce.*

Parsley Sauce

1 can condensed CREAM OF CELERY SOUP
1/2 cup MILK
2 Tbsp. PARSLEY, chopped

Combine undiluted soup and milk. Stir over low heat until hot. Add parsley.

Baked Beef Short Ribs

4 lean BEEF SHORT RIBS
1 Tbsp. BUTTER
1 med. ONION, chopped
1 cup chopped CELERY
1 tsp. SALT

1/8 tsp. PEPPER
4 med. CARROTS,
    sliced thin
1/2 tsp. fresh THYME
1/8 tsp. fresh SAGE

Trim fat from ribs. Brown beef in butter in heavy skillet or Dutch oven. While browning, add half of the onion, celery, salt and pepper. When brown, cover beef with remaining vegetables. Sprinkle with remaining salt, pepper, thyme and sage. Cover tightly. Bake in 275° oven for 3 hours or until tender. Serves 2.

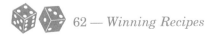

Domino Chicken Casserole

3 lbs. CHICKEN pieces
1 cup FLOUR
SALT and PEPPER
1/2 cup COOKING OIL
1 can (6 oz.) TOMATO SAUCE
4 GREEN ONIONS, chopped fine
3 cloves GARLIC, chopped fine
1 Tbsp. BARBECUE SPICES
3/4 tsp. CHILI POWDER
1/4 tsp. BASIL
1/4 tsp. CELERY SALT
1 1/3 cups WATER
2 Tbsp. WORCESTERSHIRE SAUCE
Dash TABASCO®

Combine flour, salt and pepper and dredge chicken pieces. Brown in hot oil. Combine remaining ingredients in bowl. Place chicken in casserole dish and pour sauce over all. Cover and bake in 350° oven for one hour, or until tender. For crispy crust, remove cover during last half hour of cooking.

Sherried Pot Roast

4 to 5 lb. POT ROAST
SALT and PEPPER
1/4 cup OIL
1 ONION, chopped
3 cloves GARLIC, minced
1/2 cup SHERRY

Season meat with salt and pepper, then sear in hot oil. Add onions and garlic and cook until they are wilted. Sprinkle the meat with the sherry, turning constantly. Add water, cover and cook very slowly. Repeat sprinkling with sherry until all is used. Cook slowly for two hours, or until tender. Serves 4 to 6.

Jacks or Better Rib Steaks

4 boneless RIB STEAKS
1 cup chopped TOMATOES
1/2 cup coarsely chopped ONIONS
1 can (4 oz.) diced GREEN CHILES
1 Tbsp. OLIVE OIL
1 Tbsp. VINEGAR
1 tsp. ground CORIANDER
1/4 tsp. SALT
1/4 tsp. PEPPER

Trim most of outside fat from steak. Keep refrigerated until ready to barbecue. Combine salsa ingredients and chill. Serve very cold with steaks. Makes 2 cups salsa.

Turkey Casserole

2 1/2 lbs. TURKEY
    DRUMSTICKS
1/4 cup FLOUR
1/2 tsp. PAPRIKA
1/4 tsp. PEPPER
1 tsp. SALT

1 tsp. ground GINGER
2 stalks CELERY, diced
1 ONION, sliced
1 Tbsp. BUTTER
1 1/2 cups ORANGE JUICE
3 Tbsp. SHERRY

Combine flour and seasonings and coat drumsticks. Put celery and onions in greased casserole and top with legs dotted with butter. Combine juice and sherry and pour over drumsticks. Cover and bake at 350° for 2 1/2 hours or until tender. Serve extra sauce over biscuits or rice.

Ground Turkey Meatloaf

2 lbs. freshly ground TURKEY
1 cup BREAD CRUMBS
2 EGGS, slightly beaten
1 med. ONION, minced
1/4 cup minced GREEN PEPPER
2 Tbsp. HORSERADISH
2 tsp. SALT
1 tsp. DRY MUSTARD
1/4 cup EVAPORATED MILK
3/4 cup CATSUP

Mix all ingredients (except 1/2 cup catsup) lightly. Place in 9 x 5 x 3 loaf pan. Layer top of loaf with remaining catsup. Bake at 375° for 1 1/4 hours.

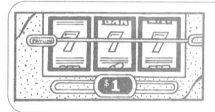

SLOT MACHINES — When playing the progressive machines be sure to play the maximum number of coins allowed on each play.

High Card Sherry Glazed Ham

1 (2-inch) center cut HAM SLICE, cooked
2 tsp. DRY MUSTARD
1/3 cup HONEY
1/2 cup SHERRY

Trim ham and score fat. Rub with dry mustard, using one teaspoon mustard on each side. Place in shallow baking pan. Combine honey and wine and pour over ham. Bake uncovered, in preheated oven at 350° for 35 minutes.

Main Dishes — 65

Atlantic City Seafood Newburg

3 Tbsp. BUTTER
2 cups fresh or canned LOBSTER, CRAB or SHRIMP
SALT
PAPRIKA
1/2 cup SHERRY
2 EGG YOLKS
1/2 cup CREAM

Melt butter in saucepan. Add seafood, season with salt and paprika and sauté gently for 5 minutes. Add wine and simmer 5 minutes. Beat egg yolks and cream together. Add to seafood mixture and cook, stirring gently, just to thicken. Serve on hot toast tips.

ROULETTE — In American roulette, the dealer usually spins the wheel, drops the ball, makes change, and collects and pays off all bets.

Oyster Casserole

1/4 lb. BUTTER, melted
1/2 lb. MUSHROOMS, sliced
2 ONIONS, chopped
2 cups BREAD CRUMBS
1 qt. OYSTERS, with juice
1/2 pt. CREAM

Melt butter in skillet. Sauté onions and mushrooms until golden. Layer oysters, onions and mushrooms in greased baking dish, covering each layer with cream. Top with bread crumbs, dot with butter and bake uncovered in 300° oven for 50 to 60 minutes.

Southwestern Shrimp Jambalaya

1 cup CELERY, sliced
2 cups RED BELL PEPPER, diced
2 med. ONIONS, sliced thin
4 Tbsp. BUTTER
2 cloves GARLIC, crushed
1 lb. HAM, cooked and cubed
2 lbs. SHRIMP, deveined and peeled
1/2 tsp. TABASCO® SAUCE
1/2 tsp. CHILI POWDER
1 tsp. SUGAR
2 cans (15 oz. ea.) whole TOMATOES
3 cups RICE, cooked

In a large Dutch oven or skillet, sauté celery, bell pepper and onions in 2 tablespoons of butter. Add garlic and ham and cook another 5 minutes. Add remaining butter, shrimp, Tabasco sauce, chili powder and sugar. Continue cooking until shrimp are done, stirring frequently. Add tomatoes and rice. Serve hot. Serves 8

Southwestern Salmon

Place **SALMON** in single layer in glass baking dish. Top with **SALSA** of choice. Bake in 350° oven, uncovered, until salmon is thoroughly cooked but not dry. Serve with lime wedges.

Filet of Sole Florentine

1/4 cup BUTTER
1/4 cup FLOUR
1 cup MILK
1/4 cup CREAM
1/2 cup CHABLIS
1 can (4 1/2 oz.) sliced MUSHROOMS
1/4 cup grated PARMESAN CHEESE
1/2 tsp. WORCESTERSHIRE SAUCE
SALT and PEPPER
2 pkgs. (10 oz. ea.) frozen SPINACH
1 1/2 lb. FILET OF SOLE

In a saucepan, melt butter and stir in flour. Add milk, cream, wine and liquid from mushrooms. Cook, stirring constantly, until mixture is thick. Add mushrooms, cheese, Worcestershire sauce, salt and pepper. Thaw spinach and spread evenly over the bottom of a 8 x 12 x 2, greased baking dish. Lay filets on top of spinach and cover with wine-cream sauce. Bake for 25 minutes at 375° or until fish flakes when tested with fork. Serves 4.

Slots o' Fun Fried Oysters

1 cup DRY BREAD CRUMBS
1 tsp. SALT
1/2 tsp. GARLIC SALT

1 pt. OYSTER MEAT
1 EGG
2 Tbsp. WATER

Combine crumbs and seasonings. Wash oysters, drain, and dry thoroughly. Dip oysters in crumbs, then into egg combined with water and again into crumbs. Fry lightly for a few minutes in hot shortening. Serve with *Tartar Sauce.*

Tartar Sauce

1 cup MAYONNAISE • 1/2 tsp. ONION JUICE • LEMON JUICE

Combine all ingredients, thinning to desired consistency with lemon juice.

Split a Pair Poached Fish

2 lbs. FISH FILETS
2 cups BOILING WATER
1/4 cup LEMON JUICE
1 sm. ONION, thinly sliced
1 tsp. SALT
3 PEPPERCORNS
2 sprigs PARSLEY
1 BAY LEAF
EGG SAUCE
PAPRIKA

Remove skin and bones from fish and cut into serving-size portions. Place fish in well-greased 10-inch frying pan. Add the next 7 ingredients. Cover and simmer 5 to 10 minutes or until fish flakes easily. Remove to heated platter. Top with *Parslied Egg Sauce,* sprinkle with paprika and serve. Serves 6.

Parslied Egg Sauce

1/4 cup BUTTER	dash PEPPER
2 Tbsp. FLOUR	1 1/4 cups MILK
3/4 tsp. DRY MUSTARD	2 EGGS, hard boiled, chopped
1/2 tsp. SALT	1 Tbsp. chopped PARSLEY

Melt butter, stir in flour and seasonings. Add milk gradually, and cook until thick and smooth. Stir constantly. Add eggs and parsley, stir and continue cooking for about 5 minutes.

BLACKJACK — If you're planning to split a pair, slide a second bet equal to the first into your betting box.

Burgundy Swiss Steak

2 lb. thick ROUND STEAK
GARLIC, SALT and PAPRIKA
3 Tbsp. FLOUR
SHORTENING
1/2 cup BURGUNDY
1 can (10 1/2 oz.) condensed ONION SOUP

Cut steak into 6 serving pieces. Sprinkle with garlic, salt and paprika and thoroughly rub with flour. Brown slowly on both sides in heated shortening. Drain off excess fat and sprinkle in any remaining flour. Add wine and soup. Cover and simmer about 1 1/2 hours or until tender. Serves 6.

Beat the House Beef Casserole

1 lb. STEWING BEEF, cut into 2-inch pieces
1/2 cup BURGUNDY
1 can (10 1/2 oz.) condensed CONSOMMÉ
3/4 tsp. SALT
1/8 tsp. PEPPER
1 med ONION, sliced
1/4 cup DRY BREAD CRUMBS, mashed fine
1/4 cup ALL PURPOSE FLOUR, sifted

Combine beef, wine, consommé, salt, pepper and onion in casserole dish. Mix flour with crumbs and stir into beef mixture. Cover and bake in at 300° for about 3 hours or until meat is tender. Serves 4.

Curried Chicken

2 pkgs. (10 oz. ea.) frozen BROCCOLI
4 CHICKEN BREASTS
buttered BREAD CRUMBS

Cover chicken breasts with water and simmer until tender. Remove chicken and cool, reserving 1 1/2 cups broth. Debone and cut chicken into serving size pieces. Place a layer of thawed broccoli in bottom of greased casserole (reserve four to six pieces for garnish). Add layer of chicken then broccoli and again chicken. Repeat layers ending with chicken on top. Pour **Curry Sauce** over all. Top with reserved broccoli and buttered bread crumbs. Bake uncovered at 350° for 45 minutes. Serves 4.

Curry Sauce

1/2 cup melted BUTTER
1/2 tsp. CURRY POWDER
1 tsp. SALT
6 Tbsp. FLOUR
1 1/2 cups CHICKEN BROTH
1 1/2 cups MILK
1 tsp. LEMON JUICE
3/4 cup MAYONNAISE

Melt butter in 3-quart saucepan. Combine curry powder and salt in flour and blend with melted butter. Add broth, milk, lemon juice and mayonnaise. Bring to boiling point, stirring constantly. Reduce heat and simmer, while stirring, for 5 minutes. Mixture will thicken to a rich, smooth sauce.

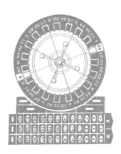

Craps Table Layout

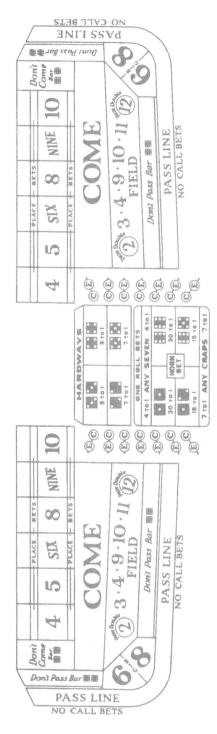

See Craps Table Glossary of Terms (Page 42)

 72 — *Winning Recipes*

Side Dishes

Cash Out Cheese Potato Casserole

6 cups cooked and sliced POTATOES
2 cups shredded CHEDDAR CHEESE
2 EGGS, beaten
1 1/2 cups MILK
2 tsp. SALT
1/8 tsp. NUTMEG

In a casserole dish, layer half of the potatoes and top with half of the cheese. Repeat layers. Combine eggs, milk, salt and nutmeg in a bowl. Pour egg mixture over contents of casserole dish and bake for 30 minutes.

Double Down!

BLACKJACK — When Doubling Down, you may wager an amount equal to your original bet. You will then receive one more card from the dealer.

Double Zero Zucchini

2 lbs. ZUCCHINI, peeled and sliced
2 TOMATOES, diced
1 ONION, thinly sliced
1 1/2 tsp. SALT
1/2 tsp. PEPPER
1/2 tsp. dried BASIL
1/2 tsp. OREGANO
3 Tbsp. BUTTER

Place zucchini, tomatoes and onion in center of large square of heavy-duty aluminum foil (or 2 layers of regular foil). Sprinkle with spices. Dot with butter. Wrap foil over vegetables and seal tightly. Cook on grill at medium heat, shaking occasionally, for 30 to 40 minutes.

Orange Rice

1/2 cup chopped ONIONS
2 Tbsp. BUTTER
5 Tbsp. concentrated frozen ORANGE JUICE
2 Tbsp. DRY VERMOUTH
1 tsp. SALT
1/4 tsp. BLACK PEPPER
1/4 tsp. CINNAMON
1 cup RICE
2 cups WATER

Bring rice and water to a boil, turn heat to low, and cook 15 minutes. Keep hot. Sauté onions in butter until tender. Add orange juice concentrate, vermouth and seasonings. Heat thoroughly. Pour over rice and toss lightly until well combined. Let stand at least 10 minutes before serving so flavors will blend. Serves 6.

SLOT MACHINES — Some say that if a machine doesn't pay off within the first ten tries — move on! But don't be surprised if the next person at that machine hits a jackpot!

Brown Rice Roulette

1 cup sliced GREEN ONIONS
2 Tbsp. VEGETABLE OIL
3 cups cooked BROWN RICE
2 Tbsp. SOY SAUCE

Sauté onions in oil until tender. Add rice and cook, stirring constantly, until rice is thoroughly heated. Stir in soy sauce.

Two Pair Potato Casserole

4 POTATOES
1/2 lb. grated AMERICAN CHEESE
1 cup MAYONNAISE
1/2 cup chopped ONIONS
SALT and PEPPER to taste
1/4 lb. partially fried BACON, chopped
1/8 cup GREEN OLIVES, sliced

Boil potatoes in skins 15 to 20 minutes or until cooked but not mushy. Drain, peel and cube potatoes and place in a large bowl. Gently fold in cheese, mayonnaise, onions, salt and pepper. Layer in a greased baking dish and top with bacon and olives. Bake at 325° for 1 hour. Serves 4.

BLACKJACK — If your first two cards add up to eight, nine, ten, or eleven, you may want to place a "double down" bet. Place the additional chips alongside the original bet and tell the dealer of your intentions.

Super Corn Casserole

1 can (16 oz.) CREAMED CORN
2 EGGS, slightly beaten
1 cup MILK
1 cup crushed SODA CRACKERS
2 1/2 Tbsp. SUGAR
3 1/2 Tbsp. melted BUTTER

Combine all ingredients and bake in greased baking dish at 350° for 1 to 1 1/2 hours or until knife inserted in middle comes out clean. Serves 4.

Inside Straight Escalloped Pumpkin

1/2 med. PUMPKIN
1 sm. ONION, finely chopped
1 GREEN BELL PEPPER, finely chopped
2 Tbsp. BUTTER
SALT, PEPPER and PAPRIKA to taste
2 oz. BUTTERED BREAD CRUMBS

Steam and mash pumpkin and place in a large bowl. Sauté onion and pepper in butter. Add to pumpkin and mix in seasonings. Place mixture in greased baking dish and sprinkle with bread crumbs. Bake at 325° for 20 minutes. Serves 4.

VIDEO POKER—*Hold* all but one nine and *draw* for the inside straight?

Baked Chiles & Onions

6 lg. WHITE ONIONS, sliced
2 sm. JALAPEÑOS, peeled, seeded and thinly sliced
2 Tbsp. BUTTER
3 Tbsp. FLOUR
1 cup MILK
3/4 cup slivered ALMONDS

Separate onions into rings, cover with lightly salted water in a saucepan and boil gently until tender. Drain and set aside. Melt butter in medium skillet, stir in flour and slowly add milk to make a cream sauce. Add jalapeños and almonds to cream sauce and remove from heat. Layer onions in a lightly buttered casserole dish, pour sauce over all and bake at 350° for 30 to 45 minutes or until casserole is set and lightly browned on top. Serves 4.

Cauliflower Soufflé

1 head CAULIFLOWER, sliced
1/4 cup diced ONION
1/2 tsp. SALT
1/2 tsp. PEPPER
1/4 tsp. NUTMEG
dash of CAYENNE
1/4 cup BUTTER

1/4 cup FLOUR
1 1/2 cups HOT MILK
5 EGGS, separated
1 3/4 cup grated SWISS
   CHEESE
1/4 cup BREAD CRUMBS
1/4 cup chopped PARSLEY

Steam cauliflower and onion until tender. In a blender, purée cauliflower, onions and spices. In a skillet, melt butter and sprinkle in the flour, cooking until lightly browned. Slowly add hot milk, stirring constantly until mixture thickens. Remove from heat and add egg yolks, one at a time, stirring well. Mix in cauliflower purée and 1 1/2 cups of the cheese. Beat all of the egg whites (add a pinch of salt) until stiff and fold into cauliflower mixture. Pour into a buttered soufflé dish and top with remaining cheese, bread crumbs and parsley. Bake at 400° for 40 minutes.

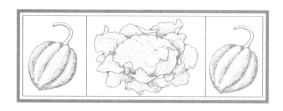

Orange-Acorn Squash

3 ACORN SQUASH
6 Tbsp. BROWN SUGAR
3 Tbsp. BUTTER

1 Tbsp. grated ORANGE PEEL
3 med. ORANGES, peeled
   and sectioned

Wash squash, cut in half crosswise and remove seeds. Place cut side down in shallow baking pan. Bake at 375° for 40 minutes. Turn cut side up and add remaining ingredients divided evenly between all. Continue baking until squash is tender, basting with melted butter and juice from bottom of pan.

Lucky Vegetable Medley

1 med. ONION, chopped
1 lg. CARROT, thinly sliced
1 stalk CELERY, thinly sliced
1 cup chopped BROCCOLI
1/2 cup CAULIFLOWER florets
1 can (8 oz.) sliced WATER
   CHESTNUTS

1/2 cup BEAN SPROUTS
4 Tbsp. SESAME OIL
3 Tbsp. VINEGAR
3 Tbsp. SUGAR
3 Tbsp. SOY SAUCE
4 Tbsp. SESAME SEEDS,
   toasted

Steam onion, carrots, celery, broccoli and cauliflower. Drain and place in a serving bowl. Add water chestnuts and bean sprouts. Place oil, vinegar, sugar and soy sauce in a saucepan and bring to a boil over high heat, stirring constantly. Remove from heat and stir into vegetable mixture, coating evenly. Garnish with sesame seeds. Serves 4.

Sweet Potato Bake

4 lg. SWEET POTATOES
1 tsp. SALT
1/3 cup SUGAR
1 3/4 tsp. PUMPKIN PIE SPICE
1/4 cup BUTTER

1 1/2 tsp. grated
   ORANGE PEEL
1 1/2 cups MILK
2 EGGS, lightly beaten

Wash sweet potatoes, place in saucepan and cover with water. Add several dashes salt, cover and boil until potatoes are tender. Peel and mash potatoes while hot. Add remaining ingredients. Pour into buttered one-quart casserole. Bake in preheated oven at 300° for 1 1/2 hours. Serves 4 to 6.

Winning Poker Hands

There are two ways to win at a poker table. The first, and most usual, is to hold the best hand at the end of play, called the "showdown". The second, is to force all competition out of the game before the showdown by raising the bet until everyone else quits.

In all games in which no wild card is used a **royal flush** is the highest ranking of all hands. The royal flush consists of 5 cards of the same suit ranking ace, king, queen, jack, and ten.

The second best hand is a **straight flush.** All of the cards must be of the same suit and sequentially numbered. An eight, seven, six, five and four of clubs is one example. A straight flush may also include an ace, ie: ace, two, three, four, and five.

Four of a kind is the next highest hand. In this case, you must have four cards of equal rank from the four different suits, ie: 4 sixes, 4 sevens etc. If you hold 4 sixes and your opponent 4 sevens, your opponent wins.

A **full house** ranks 4th. In this hand, you must have three cards of the same rank, plus two other cards of the same rank. ie: 3 kings and two sevens. In the case of two full house hands at the end of play, the highest three of a kind hand wins.

A **Flush** hand contains five cards that are all of the same suit, but not in sequential order. The cards in an "ace-high" flush would be; ace, jack, seven, four and three all of the same suit.

Straights are five cards that are sequential, but not of the same suit. For instance: a 10 of diamonds, 9 of clubs, 8 of spades, 7 of hearts and 6 of spades would be a ten-high straight.

Three of a kind hands contain three cards of the same rank ie. 10 of diamonds, 10 of spades, and 10 of hearts.

Two pair hands contain two sets of cards that are of the same rank, ie: 2 sevens and 2 tens.

One pair hands contain one set of cards of the same rank, ie: 2 jacks or 2 fours.

No pair hands are the lowest of all hands. In this case, the hand holding the single highest card is the winner.

A
♦

Desserts & Drinks

No Gamble Pecan Pie

1/2 cup HONEY
1/2 cup BROWN SUGAR
1/4 cup BUTTER
3 EGGS, beaten
1 cup PECANS
1 (9-inch) unbaked PIE SHELL

Blend honey and sugar together. Cook slowly to form a smooth syrup. Add butter, beaten eggs and pecans. Pour into pie shell and bake at 400° for 8 to 10 minutes. Reduce oven heat to 350° and bake for 30 minutes more, or until tests done.

Honey-Date Bars

1 cup HONEY
1/2 cup SHORTENING
1 tsp. VANILLA
3 EGGS
1 1/4 cup FLOUR

1 tsp. BAKING POWDER
1/2 tsp. SALT
1 cup chopped DATES
1 cup NUT MEATS
POWDERED SUGAR

Blend shortening, honey and vanilla until creamy. Beat in eggs one at a time. Blend in sifted dry ingredients. Add nuts and dates and stir just enough to distribute evenly. Spread in greased 9 x 9 baking pan and bake at 350° for 30 to 35 minutes. Cool, cut into one-inch bars and roll in powdered sugar. Makes about 3 dozen bars.

Lemon Meringue Pie

1 cup WATER
3/4 cup SUGAR
1/4 tsp. SALT
1 tsp. grated LEMON RIND
5 Tbsp. CORNSTARCH
1/2 cup COLD WATER

3 EGG YOLKS
1 Tbsp. BUTTER
6 Tbsp. LEMON JUICE
1 (8-inch) unbaked PIE
   SHELL

Combine water, sugar, salt and lemon rind in saucepan and bring to a boil. Add cornstarch which has been blended with water. Cook over low heat until thickened (about 5 minutes), stirring constantly. Remove from heat. Add well-beaten egg yolks, then the butter and finally the lemon juice, mixing well after each addition. Pour into pie shell and top with *Lemon Meringue*.

Lemon Meringue

3 EGG WHITES
1/4 tsp. CREAM OF TARTAR
Dash of SALT

9 Tbsp. SUGAR
1 tsp. LEMON JUICE

Beat egg whites until stiff (but not dry). Sprinkle with cream of tartar and salt and beat lightly. Add sugar slowly by tablespoons (beating thoroughly to dissolve sugar grains). Fold in lemon juice. Swirl meringue on top of pie, bringing to outer rim of pastry (to prevent shrinkage). Bake at 325° for 15 minutes (on middle shelf). Open oven door slightly and allow pie to cool slowly. While meringue is slightly warm, cut with heated knife. Chill and serve.

Winning Walnut Pie

1/2 cup BROWN SUGAR, packed
2 Tbsp. all-purpose FLOUR
1 1/4 cups LIGHT CORN SYRUP
3 Tbsp. BUTTER
1/4 tsp. SALT
3 EGGS
1 1/2 tsp. VANILLA
1 cup WALNUTS, chopped
1 (9-inch) uncooked PIE SHELL

Mix brown sugar and flour in saucepan. Add corn syrup, butter and salt, and warm over low heat just until butter is melted. In a large bowl, beat eggs with vanilla. Stir in sugar mixture. Pour into pie shell and sprinkle with walnuts. Bake on lower rack of oven at 350° for 40 to 45 minutes (until filling is set at center). Cool before cutting.

Strawberry Glazed Plum Pie

1 pkg. (8 oz.) CREAM CHEESE, softened
1/3 cup SUGAR
Juice and grated rind of 1/2 ORANGE
1 (8-inch) baked PIE SHELL
1 1/2 cups fresh PLUMS, sliced

In a bowl, whip cream cheese with sugar, grated orange rind and orange juice. Spread cream cheese mixture in cooled pie shell. Arrange plum slices on cream cheese mixture. Pour *Strawberry Glaze* over top. Chill before serving.

Strawberry Glaze

1 cup crushed STRAWBERRIES
1/4 cup CURRANT JELLY
1 Tbsp. CORNSTARCH

In a saucepan, combine strawberries, jelly and cornstarch. Cook over low heat, stirring constantly, until sauce thickens.

Bonanza Fudge Pie

1/4 lb. BUTTER or MARGARINE
2 squares BAKING CHOCOLATE
2 EGGS
1 cup SUGAR
1/4 cup FLOUR

Melt butter or margarine in medium saucepan. Add chocolate and stir until melted. Add eggs, sugar and flour. Combine well. Pour into buttered pie pan. Bake at 350° for 30 minutes. Cool before cutting. Serve with ice cream and chocolate sauce.

ROULETTE — Cover all of the numbers in the red and black squares and you still lose if that little white ball drops into the zero or double zero slot.

Chocolate Cheesecake

1 pkg. CHOCOLATE CAKE MIX
4 EGGS
1/3 cup BUTTER, softened
1 pkg. (16 oz.) CREAM CHEESE, softened
2 tsp. VANILLA EXTRACT
3/4 cup SUGAR

In a large bowl, combine cake mix, butter and 1 egg. Pour into 9 x 13 baking pan. Beat cream cheese, eggs, vanilla and sugar until smooth. Spread over cake mix. Bake at 350° for 25 to 30 minutes. Frost if desired. Chill at least 12 hours before slicing.

Raisin Cheesecake with Cinnamon Crumb Crust

4 EGGS
1 cup SUGAR
1/4 tsp. SALT
1 1/2 lbs. (3 cups) RICOTTA
     CHEESE
1 cup WHIPPING CREAM
4 Tbsp. all-purpose FLOUR
1 tsp. VANILLA
3 Tbsp. LEMON JUICE
1 Tbsp. grated LEMON PEEL
1/2 cup SEEDLESS RAISINS

In a large mixing bowl, beat eggs until light-colored. Gradually add sugar, beating until mixture is thick and light. Thoroughly beat in salt and ricotta then the cream. Beat in flour, vanilla and lemon juice. Fold in lemon peel and raisins. Pour over cooled *Cinnamon Crumb Crust* and sprinkle top with reserved crumbs. Bake at 350° for 1 hour and 10 minutes (or until toothpick inserted in center comes out clean). Turn oven off, leave door open and allow cake to cool for about 2 hours. Cover and chill in spring-form pan.

Cinnamon Crumb Crust

1 pkg. (6 oz.) ZWIEBACK
1/2 cup SUGAR
1/2 tsp. CINNAMON
1/3 cup BUTTER, melted

Crush zwieback in blender or by hand into fine crumbs. Mix well with sugar, cinnamon and melted butter. Set aside 3/4 cup of the crumb mixture and press the balance firmly over bottom of a 9-inch spring-form pan. Bake at 350° for 15 minutes or until lightly browned. Cool.

Peanut Butter-Orange Cake

2 2/3 cups FLOUR, sifted
1 cup SUGAR
2 tsp. BAKING SODA
3/4 tsp. CINNAMON
1/4 tsp. SALT
2/3 cup BROWN SUGAR, packed
1 cup PEANUT BUTTER
2 EGGS
1 1/3 cups ORANGE JUICE
1 ORANGE
1/3 cup BROWN SUGAR, packed

Sift first five ingredients together into a large bowl. Add brown sugar, peanut butter, eggs and orange juice. Stir slightly to mix, then beat until batter is smooth (med. speed with mixer, 100 times by hand).

Peel orange and grate one tablespoon of peel. Cut orange into fine pieces and drain. Stir orange pieces and peel into batter. Pour batter into greased and floured 13 x 9 x 2 cake pan. Sprinkle 1/3 cup brown sugar evenly over top of batter. Bake at 325° for 45 to 50 minutes.

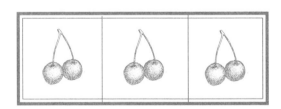

SLOT MACHINES —About 80% of first-time casino visitors head for the slots. In addition to being easy to play, the slots offer some of the largest, most lifestyle-changing jackpots.

Las Vegas Cookies

1 cup BUTTER
2 cups BROWN SUGAR
3 EGGS
1/4 cup HONEY
1 tsp. BRANDY EXTRACT
1 tsp. VANILLA
3 1/2 cups FLOUR
1 tsp. BAKING SODA
1 tsp. CINNAMON
1/2 tsp. CLOVES
1/2 tsp. NUTMEG
1 cup WHITE RAISINS
1 cup DATES, chopped
1 cup FRUIT CAKE FRUIT MIX
1 cup NUTS, chopped
1/4 cup LEMON JUICE

Cream butter and sugar. Add eggs, one at a time, beating until fluffy. Add honey and extracts. Blend until smooth. Mix dry ingredients together. Add to sugar mixture and mix until all are well blended. Add raisins, dates, fruits and nuts. Add lemon juice last. Drop by spoonfuls onto cookie sheet and bake at 350° for 20 minutes or until golden brown. Makes 6 dozen cookies.

DID YOU KNOW — In 1931 the Nevada legislature passed a bill making gambling legal in the state?

Breakfast Bracer

2 EGG YOLKS, beaten
juice of 4 ORANGES

2 tsp. HONEY
pinch of SALT

Combine ingredients, beating thoroughly. Serves 2.

Orange-Carrot Drink

1 1/2 cups ORANGE JUICE
1 1/2 cups MILK
2 CARROTS, cut small
1/4 cup HONEY

Combine all ingredients in blender
and process until smooth. Serves 4.

DID YOU KNOW — The two biggest factors fueling the rise in casino gambling in recent years has been the legalization of riverboat gambling in certain states and the many Indian tribes that have begun to offer gaming on their reservations.

Instant Breakfast in a Mug

6 Tbsp. frozen ORANGE JUICE, concentrate
3/4 cup COLD WATER
1 cup MILK
1/2 BANANA
1 cup CORN FLAKES
1 EGG
1 Tbsp. SUGAR

Combine~all ingredients in blender and process at high speed until smooth.. Serves 2.

Spiced Coffee

4 cups WATER
1/3 cup DARK BROWN SUGAR
4 rounded tsp. INSTANT COFFEE
4 CINNAMON STICKS

Combine water and sugar in medium saucepan. Bring to a boil and stir until sugar is dissolved. Reduce heat to simmer, stir in coffee and simmer 1 to 2 minutes. Pour into mugs and add cinnamon sticks. Serves 4.

Lucky Party Cherry Delight

1 pkg. CHERRY KOOL AID®
1 pkg. RASPBERRY COOL AID®
2 cups SUGAR
2 qts. WATER
1 can (46 oz.) UNSWEETENED
    PINEAPPLE JUICE
2 qt. GINGER ALE

Combine all ingredients (except ginger ale) and chill. At serving time, pour into punch bowl and add ginger ale. Makes 50 punch cup servings.

Bloody Mary

1 1/4 cups TOMATO JUICE
1 can (12 oz.) V-8® JUICE
1 1/2 tsp. WORCESTERSHIRE SAUCE
1/4 tsp. TABASCO® SAUCE
1/2 tsp. CELERY SALT
VODKA

Combine and blend on low speed in blender. Chill well. Serve with 1 part vodka for every 2 parts mix. Serves 4.

Chocolate Cooler

1 1/4 cups WATER
1 tsp. SUGAR
1 tsp. CINNAMON
2 qts. CHOCOLATE MILK

Combine 1/2 cup water, sugar and cinnamon. Boil one minute. Add remaining water, pour into ice cube trays and freeze. To serve: place cubes in cups or glasses filled with chocolate milk.

Sunshine Shake

1 can (6 oz.) frozen, concen-
    trated ORANGE JUICE
1 cup MILK
2 cups VANILLA ICE CREAM

Combine all ingredients and blend thoroughly. Serves 8.

Strawberry-Chocolate Delight

2 med. BANANAS
3 cups cold MILK
1 pkg. (10 oz.) sliced FROZEN STRAWBERRIES,
    thawed, or, 1 1/4 cups sliced FRESH STRAWBERRIES
1 1/2 pts. CHOCOLATE ICE CREAM

Blend bananas, milk, strawberries (sweetened to taste) and 1/2 pint of the ice cream. Blend until smooth. Pour into tall chilled glasses and top each with a scoop of ice cream.

Banana-Pineapple Breakfast

1 BANANA
1 1/2 cups PINEAPPLE JUICE
1 EGG
1/2 cup MILK
4 ICE CUBES

Mix ingredients in blender until ice is thoroughly crushed. Serve immediately. Serves 2.

Lemon-Orange Cooler

1 qt. WATER
2 cups SUGAR

1 1/2 tsp. grated LEMON PEEL
1 pt. ORANGE JUICE

Combine water and sugar in saucepan, bring to a boil, and boil for 10 minutes. Steep lemon peel in sugar syrup, strain and add lemon juice. Cool and add orange juice. Chill and serve. Serves 4.

Orange Shrub

1 pt. LEMON SHERBET
1/2 cup APRICOT PRESERVES
1 can (6 oz.) frozen ORANGE JUICE, concentrate

Soften sherbet and blend with preserves. Stir in thawed orange concentrate. Fill 8 large glasses with crushed ice. Add orange mixture and stir.

Hot Mocha

2 cups MILK
2 tsp. INSTANT CHOCOLATE
2 tsp. INSTANT COFFEE

WHIPPED CREAM
CINNAMON

Heat milk in a saucepan over low heat. Stir in chocolate and coffee until thoroughly combined. Serve in mugs with a dollop of whipped cream and a sprinkle of cinnamon.

Café Royale Flush

1 mug COFFEE • 1/2 oz. BRANDY • LEMON PEEL

Add brandy to coffee and sweeten to taste. Add small twist of lemon peel and serve.

Café Brûlot

1 ORANGE PEEL, cut into thin strips
4 sticks CINNAMON
2 whole CLOVES
6 cubes SUGAR
1/2 cup BRANDY
4 cups COFFEE, double-strength

Make coffee and pour into serving carafe. Place orange rind in a shallow heat-resistant dish and add cinnamon, cloves, sugar cubes and warmed brandy. Light with a match. Stir until flames die down and sugar is melted. Add to hot coffee and serve. Makes one-quart.

Jackpot Party Punch

2 cups sliced fresh PEACHES
2 cups MELON BALLS
2 cups STRAWBERRIES, halved
1/4 cup SUGAR
1 Tbsp. LEMON JUICE
2 bottles (4/5 qt. ea.) CHABLIS
2 bottles (4/5 qt. ea.)
    CHAMPAGNE

Combine fruits, sugar, lemon juice and wine. Refrigerate several hours. Pour into chilled punch bowl over a small block of ice. Add chilled champagne. Serves 30.

Super Slot Payoff Punch

1/2 cup SUGAR
3/4 cup WATER
6 strips LEMON PEEL
12 CLOVES
3-inch STICK CINNAMON
1 cup ORANGE JUICE
1/2 cup LEMON JUICE
1 cup CANNED PEAR JUICE
1 pint BRANDY
1 1/2 cup SPARKLING WATER

Boil sugar, water, lemon peel, cloves and cinnamon for five minutes. Cool and strain. Add remainder of ingredients. Pour over a small block of ice in chilled punch bowl and garnish with fruit. Serves 6.

SALSA LOVERS COOK BOOK

More than 180 taste-tempting recipes for salsas that will make every meal a special event! Salsas for salads, appetizers, main dishes, and desserts! Put some salsa in your life! By Susan K. Bollin.

5 1/2 x 8 1/2—128 pages . . . $5.95

CHIP & DIP LOVERS COOK BOOK

More than 150 recipes for fun and festive dips. Make southwestern dips, dips with fruits and vegetables, meats, poultry and seafood. Salsa dips and dips for desserts. Includes recipes for making homemade chips. By Susan K. Bollin.

5 1/2 x 8 1/2—112 pages . . . $5.95

QUICK-N-EASY MEXICAN RECIPES

More than 175 favorite Mexican recipes you can prepare in less than thirty minutes. Traditional items such as tacos, tostadas and enchiladas. Also features easy recipes for salads, soups, breads, desserts and drinks. By Susan K. Bollin.

5 1/2 x 8 1/2—128 pages . . . $5.95

CHILI-LOVERS' COOK BOOK

Chili cookoff prize-winning recipes and regional favorites! The best of chili cookery, from mild to fiery, with and without beans. Plus a variety of taste-tempting foods made with chile peppers. 150,000 copies in print! By Al and Mildred Fischer.

5 1/2 x 8 1/2—128 pages . . . $5.95

TORTILLA LOVERS COOK BOOK

From tacos to tostadas, enchiladas to nachos, every dish celebrates the tortilla! More than 100 easy to prepare, festive recipes for breakfast, lunch and dinner. Filled with Southwestern flavors! By Bruce Fischer and Bobbie Salts.

5 1/2 x 8 1/2 — 112 pages . . . $6.95

ORDER BLANK

GOLDEN WEST PUBLISHERS

✸ 4113 N. Longview Ave. • Phoenix, AZ 85014

602-265-4392 • **1-800-658-5830** • FAX 602-279-6901

Qty	Title	Price	Amount
	Arizona Cook Book	**5.95**	
	Best Barbecue Recipes	**5.95**	
	Chip and Dip Cook Book	**5.95**	
	Chili-Lovers' Cook Book	**5.95**	
	Cowboy Cartoon Cook Book	**5.95**	
	Easy Recipes for Wild Game & Fish	**6.95**	
	Gourmet Gringo Cook Book	**14.95**	
	Grand Canyon Cook Book	**6.95**	
	Joy of Muffins	**5.95**	
	Mexican Desserts & Drinks	**6.95**	
	Mexican Family Favorites Cook Book	**6.95**	
	New Mexico Cook Book	**5.95**	
	Quick-n-Easy Mexican Recipes	**5.95**	
	Real New Mexico Chile Cook Book	**6.95**	
	Salsa Lovers Cook Book	**5.95**	
	Tequila Cook Book	**7.95**	
	Texas Cook Book	**5.95**	
	Tortilla Lovers Cook Book	**6.95**	
	Wholly Frijoles! The Whole Bean Cook Book	**6.95**	
	Winning Recipes	**6.95**	
Shipping & Handling Add ⮕	U.S. & Canada	$3.00	
	Other countries	$5.00	

☐ My Check or Money Order Enclosed $

☐ MasterCard   ☐ VISA ($20 credit card minimum)

(Payable in U.S. funds)

Acct. No.	Exp. Date

Signature	

Name	Telephone

Address	

City/State/Zip

Call for FREE catalog

9/97   Winning Recipes

This order blank may be photo-copied